CONSIDER THIS?!

An Entrepreneur's
Guide to Success

KEITH HERMAN

Copyright © 2023 by Keith Herman

First Edition

Consider this?! An Entrepreneur's Guide to Success

ISBN HARDCOVER: 979-8-9875795-0-3

ISBN PAPERBACK: 979-8-9875795-8-9

ISBN TRADE PAPERBACK: 979-8-9875795-9-5

ISBN EBOOK: 979-8-9875795-1-0

ISBN EPUB: 979-8-9875795-2-7

ISBN KINDLE: 979-8-9875795-3-4

ISBN NOOK: 979-8-9875795-4-1

ISBN MOBI: 979-8-9875795-5-8

ISBN EBK: 979-8-9875795-6-5

ISBN PDF: 979-8-9875795-7-2

Library of Congress Control Number: 2023900493

All rights reserved. This book may not be reproduced in whole or in part, or transmitted in any form, without written permission from the publisher, except by a reviewer who may quote brief passages in a review. Nor may any part of this book be reproduced, stored in a retrieval system, or transmitted in any form or by any means graphic, electronic, mechanical, photocopying, recording, or other, without written permission from the publisher.

Keith Publishing

3109 Grand Avenue #101, Miami, Florida 33133

Copyright, Legal Notice, and Disclaimer

This publication is protected under the US Copyright Act of 1976 and all other applicable international, federal, state, and local laws. All rights are reserved, including resale rights. If you purchased this book without a cover, you should be aware that this book is stolen property.

It was reported as "unsold" or "destroyed" to the publisher, and neither the author nor the publisher has received any payment for this" stripped book."

Please note that much of this publication is based on personal experience and anecdotal evidence. Although the author and publisher have made every reasonable attempt to achieve complete accuracy of the content in this guide, they assume no responsibility for errors or omissions. Also, you should use this information as you see fit, and at your own risk. Your particular situation may not be exactly suited to the examples illustrated here; you should adjust your use of the information and recommendations accordingly. Meant to inform and entertain the reader, nothing in this book should replace common sense, legal, medical, or other professional advice.

Any trademarks, service marks, product names, ppr name features are assumed to be the property of their respective owners and are used only for reference. There is no implied endorsement if we use these items.

For information about exclusive discounts for bulk purchases, please contact Keith Publishing at business@keithherman.com.

Editor: Jessie Raymond

Book Cover Design: umairdeveloper1

Book Cover Background: FLY:D *(https://unsplash.com/@flyd2069)*

Text & Layout Design: *Accuracy4sure@gmail.com*

Printed in the United States of America

10 9 8 7 6 5 4 3 2 1

Consider this?!

An Entrepreneur's Guide to Success

Consider this?!
An Entrepreneur's Guide to Success

<u>Inspire</u> - fill (someone) with the urge or ability to do or feel something, especially to do something creative

<u>Empower</u> - make (someone) stronger and more confident, especially in controlling their life and claiming their rights

This book is for those who want to be <u>**Empowered!**</u>

Is that you?

Enjoy!

Acknowledgments

Authoring a book is a gift! A gift most people never accept.

It is an opportunity to reflect, share with others, and effect change.

It is also an opportunity to acknowledge those who contributed to the rich and meaningful experiences shared.

The benefits of publishing a book are intangible and priceless.

Thank you to the following people that graciously shared their time, experiences, and wisdom: Jeff Abrams, Eden Alpert, Muhammad Ali, Jarvis Astaire, Sheila Baer, Adriana Balaban, Alain Bezamat, James Beriker, Stanley Black, James Branciforte, Eli Broad, Ryan Chandler Brown, Won-G Bruny, Marcia Caden, Rev. Thomas Clark, Neal Cohen, Warren Cohen, Ian Copeland, Anna Chuprina, Roy Cohn, Jason Derulo, Joe DiMaggio, Elliot Disner, Greg Ekizian, Leonard Frankel, Sheldon Fleigelman, Eric Fleishman, Alice Fleming, Robert Freidman, David Foster, Nicholas Frankl, Maurice Goldberg, Jennifer Goodenough, Sheldon Gordon, Mark Goulston, Steven Griffith, Rosalyn Gruen, Jack Guy, Richard Hartog, Mohamed Hadid, David Hawkins, Ben & Mollie Heller, Arnold Herman, Magic Johnson, Mel Katten, David Christopher Lee, Lawrence Levine, Jon Lovitz, Henrik Lundqvist, Spider Lockhart, Timothy J. Mara, Ann Manners, Bill Mark, Billie Martin, Stephen Meade, Roberto Medrano, Paula Kent Meehan, Kimberly Moore, David Moss, Joe Namath, Fabiano do Nascimento, Meghan Noone, Steve Owens, Arnold Palmer, Sanford Paul, Penney Peirce, Rocco Pirrotta, Alan Ben Porat, Chere Rachelle, Dean Radin, Robert Rautbord, Faithe Robbins, Olga Cristina Rodriguez, Mickey Rourke, Mary Carol Rudin, Jeffrey Rueben, Chirag Sagar, Mike Schenker, Rudolf Schenker, Jeffrey Schick, Robert Shmelzer Jr., Adam Shaffer, Russell Simmons, Paul

Stanley, Phu Styles, Miguel Suarez, Jack Tapp, Brad & Mandi Tinsley, Sheldon Toll, Adam Torres, Alex & Jean Trebek, Chakrapani Ullal, Stevie Ray Vaughn, Brandi Veil, Jon Voight, Mark Wahlberg, Neal Walsh, Occo Weber, Izzy Weisberg, Ronald Wesley, Dee Winston, Steve Wood, Ronnie Wood, Cheryl Woodcock, Christopher Kai Wong, Austin Yavorsky, Yoshisada Yonezuka, the anonymous woman at the café on Magazine Street in New Orleans, and countless others.

Remember:

"When the student is ready, the master will appear."

—Buddha-

Dedication

For my readers, life students, and fearless adventurers who look for a fun, exciting, rewarding, happy & successful life.

This book is for you!

Dedication

Foreword

A forward thinker, a pioneer, and a revolutionary entrepreneur. Keith Herman are all these things and more. When you read this book, you will learn how to be the same for yourself.

His business secrets and strategies for success, which he's about to share with you in this book, in summary, is to hyper-focus on your growth mindset. In the words of the famous author, Willie Jolley, **"a setback is a setup for a comeback."**

He believes your failures don't define you. You can thrive on challenges and shouldn't see failure as a way to describe yourself but rather you can learn how to use your failures as a springboard for your personal and professional growth. You will also read about fascinating scientific theories that he discovered to breakdown how you can think more decisively with confidence and clarity.

Keith will help you discover your hidden gems, the true power of your mind, the essence of leadership, and the undeniable reward you will reap when you work hard by applying his principles of success.

His wealth of information stems from his decades of business experience where he has created, built, and scaled more than 50 businesses. He has also helped his clients raise more than $500 million and, has been involved with over $2 billion in transactions.

His insights will serve as a solid foundation for your journey as an aspiring or seasoned entrepreneur for small or large-scale organizations. You'll see for yourself that you are never alone in your struggle and that when you learn from this business sage, you are always supported in spirit.

Keith will leave you in awe of how much unlimited potential you wield. When you read this book, you will understand the exact steps you can use to change your outlook on life for the better.

Your journey to greatness begins now.

Christopher Kai

Fortune 100 Global Speaker

#1 bestselling author of "Wizard of Words: The 7 Magical Words for Your Success"

Content

Acknowledgments ix

Dedication xi

Foreword xiii

Introduction 1

Chapter 1 | At least half of what people learn growing up is false 5

Chapter 2 | At this moment, you lack the awareness of knowledge or experience to reach your goal now! 25

Chapter 3 | You do not create anything. 31

Chapter 4 | If we only retain 20%, or less, of what we learn, then why spend time reading and memorizing facts & figures? 39

Chapter 5 | You spend a disproportionate amount of time thinking how to solve problems than solving problems. 53

Chapter 6 | You are not in Flow! 65

Chapter 7 | Everyone has the same single greatest challenge. 77

Chapter 8 | You have access to more knowledge than you need. 95

Chapter 9 | Skills are like tools. They work best when sharpened. 107

Chapter 10 | Life is more enjoyable having positive experiences. 115

Chapter 11 | The primary benefit of working with others is not achieving a common goal. 133

Chapter 12 | An instant of change can transform a life forever 145

Chapter 13 | Why must we always chop wood, carry water? 161

Chapter 14 | How to break barriers? 169

Chapter 15 | What does it all mean? 179

Chapter 16 | Where to start? 191

Chapter 17 | How to reach the finish line!... 199

Your Guide How to Become a Successful Entrepreneur.................. 211

Closing Thought 217

Glossary 219

Notations.. 227

Introduction

With absolute certainty, he knew he would win. How often are you 100% certain you are correct? He was confident, not overconfident. The stakes were high, $27,000,000 to be exact, and yet he did not even break a sweat. Would you?

Would you play the lottery on the condition you would win? I am not suggesting it would be as simple as filling out five or six numbers on a form and paying for the ticket.

Would you be willing to remain patient and diligent while researching for an absolute win? Would you find the nearest store to buy the tickets, drive there, fill them out, and hand over the money? It may take days, weeks, or even months. You may need to buy tickets from multiple locations and for substantial amounts of money. Would you do it if you knew you would surely win?

Of course, you would! Because you are a savvy and motivated entrepreneur. You know that nothing comes without work, and there are no better odds than 100% certainty. So, if the juice is worth the squeeze, you would certainly do it.

That is what Stefan Mandel did in 1992. Stefan was born in Romania and educated as a savvy Romanian-Australian economist. He put his education to work and bought every combination of tickets in Virginia's $27 million jackpot.

He knew he would win not only one first prize but astoundingly also six- second prizes, 132 third prizes, and thousands of lesser rewards. Ridiculous, right? But true!

Stefan had considerable experience playing lotteries since the 1950s. Before the Virginia lottery, he had won thirteen previous lotteries stretching from Romania to Australia. In a post-win interview, he said on the day of the lottery; he did not even experience an ounce of worry because he was a winner for sure.

Like any successful business, Stefan used a plan that prioritized knowledge and experience. It required substantial research, discipline, and patience. As a result, he experienced calm, certainty, and a grand payoff.

Funny enough, everything was already there for him! Yes, everything, and do not forget this! Because we will discuss this in more detail in the chapters that follow.

What if it was that simple? Would you commit to the hours, do the research, stick to the plan, and exercise patience? Knowing you will succeed; would your mindset keep you as cool as a cucumber like Stefan?

Oddly enough, I know countless people that would decline the opportunity. Most people I know would pass. I can imagine them saying there must be a trick, and they are not willing to take the risk, or only lucky people win, or money does not motivate them.

Even with proof staring them in the face that it is 100% certain they won't fork over even a dollar to win $1,000,000,000. That is just human nature and perfectly fine. Not everyone has the same motivation or mindset.

However, you are not them. You are motivated, entrepreneurial, and with goals that carry risks not palatable by most people. As an entrepreneur, you also have an open mind and willingness to change, act and transform for the rewards. And candidly, you are here to win!

My goal with this book is to share information that can change your thoughts on how to act, transform your life, and help you win the success you want. I am not talking about playing the lottery as

Stefan did. I am talking about achieving your specific entrepreneurial goal, whatever that may be.

Picture me as your coach preparing you for a race. I am here to share knowledge and to get you pumped up to instill confidence before you start the race. I want you to overcome the hurdles and watch you glide across the finish line victoriously.

No one is saying it will be quick, easy, or incident free. However, as Stefan knows, the best information will make it easier and achievable. Together, we can get you across the finish line. And remember, your success is also my success.

As we move forward, you will hear about new methodologies, controversial topics, and different processes. There is no reason to judge any of it. I suggest you keep it in mind as you read the book.

I use real-life examples to illustrate points and keep things interesting. I even play devil's advocate along the way because even I question what I read. If everything goes well, you will consider other perspectives and your mind on matters and hopefully get closer to your goals. I ask you to keep an open mind and consider this.

Chapter 1

At Least Half of What People Learn Growing Up Is False.

"Beware of false knowledge it is more dangerous than ignorance."

—George Bernard Shaw

Tears rolled down my freckled cheeks as my body uncontrollably twitched at the wretched thought of consuming what sat before me. "There is no way I'm drinking it; it's disgusting," I declared. Before I knew what hit me, I was airborne and off the left side of the chair and onto the floor. That was my dad's way of getting my attention. And, sure enough, that strategy worked for him every time.

"You are going to drink it because it is good for you. So, get off the God damn floor and get it over with before things get worse." "But it really does hurt my stomach, and I can't," I replied. "You are going to feel much worse pain if you don't," he countered. And so, I did.

Within thirty minutes, the cramps took over, and I angrily debated how to manage the encounter with this despicable liquid as I cringed through the pain. The torment went on for years until one day, when my mother produced the brilliant idea to take me to the doctor. My father commented, "there better be something wrong with you, or there will be hell to pay."

My father was always right, but I believed he was not in that case. "How could something that gives me a stomachache be good for me?" I thought. It simply made no sense. However, my father thought it was merely coincidental. It was the 70s, and medicine was far less of a science and knowledge not as easily accessible.

The doctor greeted me in the patient room and quickly had me lie on the table for an examination. He began probing around my stomach and lower intestines with short-hand compressions, asking me to describe the problem.

He went ahead professionally with his stethoscope hanging from his pocket. He glanced in different directions, contorting his face as if he were on the cusp of a grand discovery. After a minute, he gazed over to my mother and projected confidently, "he must have a sensitivity to milk. I recommend he lay off the milk for a while, and we can follow up in two months."

That is, it! I thought to myself as my heart raced. I am in big trouble! My father is never going to buy off on such a paltry explanation. It was far from an articulate diagnosis. However, it was at least something.

My mom could sense my anxiety about returning home without the bacon. So, as moms do, she assured me she would dress it up in her own words to make it incomprehensible to my father and sell it based on his ignorance. Frankly, she was most concerned about not having any more violence, so she did her best to do what she needed to keep the peace within the house.

Thirty years would pass until I visited a doctor that decided a lactose test was in order. Voila! "You are lactose intolerant," the doctor exclaimed. "Excuse me, what are you talking about?" The doctor went on to explain in more detail.

It finally vindicated me like a prisoner on death row cleared by newly discovered DNA evidence. Unfortunately, my father had long passed, so the moment was bittersweet. I did not get the "I told you so" moment, but at least I was able to erase one more uncertainty from my mind.

Can you relate to my experience? You discovered something your parents or loved one told you to be untrue. They were the ones you placed your trust in. They had no bad intentions. The information they received was passed to them the same way. It would take years for you to find the truth and then, upon learning the truth, experience disappointment or a sigh of relief.

Milk is good for you is a simple example of something they made us believe is good for you but turns out to be sometimes false. In fact, according to the National Health Institute, about 65% of the adult human population has a type of lactose intolerance, which results in abdominal pain and other gastrointestinal consequences after eating dairy products. Such a staggering number is hard to deny. Chances are, if your parents told you the same, they were wrong too.

But could it be true that as much as half of what we learn growing up is inaccurate? I mean, how could it be that so much information we receive is false? Have you ever even thought about it? And is it true for every generation? Let us delve deeper to consider this claim.

Think back to your earlier years. Think of all the things you can recall learning from your parents, siblings, grandparents, friends, and even teachers that have proven to be false. Things that may have mattered or seemed esoteric.

Did your science teacher tell you there are nine planets? Mercury, Venus, Earth, Mars, Jupiter, Saturn, Uranus, Neptune, and Pluto?

Since then, we learned Pluto is not like the other eight planets. In fact, for some time, it became declassified as a planet altogether. And after all the commotion, it is now a dwarf planet, and we still debate even that.

Were you taught the smallest particle is an atom? All solids, gases, and liquids are composed of neutral or charged atoms. They are exceedingly small and typically considered to be approximately 100 picometers in diameter. Did you know it took almost two millennia until we recognized the atom as a physical object? Remarkable!

Now, in less than 10% of that time, we have discovered something smaller called quarks. A quark is about 60,000 times smaller than the radius of a hydrogen atom. A quark is a type of elementary particle and a fundamental constituent of matter. Quarks combine to form composite particles called hadrons, the most stable of which are protons and neutrons, the components of atomic nuclei. They compose all observable matter as up quarks, down quarks, and electrons.[1]

If that was not enough, there is something unimaginably smaller called the gluon. A gluon is an elementary particle that acts as the exchange particle (or gauge boson) for the strong force between quarks. It is analogous to the exchange of photons in the electromagnetic force between two charged particles. Gluons bind quarks together, forming hadrons such as protons and neutrons.[2]

These scientific facts may seem esoteric to you. In other words, they do not affect you whatsoever. However, for people in the scientific community, these facts do matter. Because they are working on projects that can change the world and even human existence. It is analogous to reaching a dead end or a fork in the road. You realize you wasted time or need to re-think things or change direction.

Did your family or friends tell you getting money and possessions will bring happiness? Did they describe the excitement or the rush they experience when they obtain money or something new? Did they encourage you and cheer you on to make it your focus?

There are so many examples around us, and we should know better than to entertain the thought. Yet so many people continue to perpetuate this falsehood. Think about it. A man with $100,000,000 is no happier than a man with $90,000,000. Ok, so maybe I am being silly, but there is proof everywhere. For example:

James Altucher founded a Web design company called Reset Inc. in 1996 and sold it two years later for $10 million. Then, he lost everything in a series of poor investments worsened by the first tech bubble in 2000. After nearly committing suicide, Altucher said in an interview with Glenn Beck that he eventually realized he couldn't judge his "self-worth by his net worth." He turned it all around and reclaimed everything by being a hedge fund manager, and today is a successful blogger and podcast host.

Remember a guy named MC Hammer? Yes, I am referring to Stanley Kirk Burrell. He was a mega superstar in the early-1990s with his hits "U Can't Touch This" and "Too Legit to Quit." He sold 50+ million records. Despite his success, he fell into debt and by 1996 filed bankruptcy, owing more than $13 million. Nevertheless, he, too, found happiness as a Christian preacher and being of service to others. Burrell became an entrepreneur by launching record labels, investing in tech companies, and being a public figure once again. Burrell continues to share his story to empower others to achieve their dreams and true happiness.

Binance CEO ChangPeng Zhao is worth $18.5 billion and has said he does not really care much about money.' He is one of the richest figures in the world of digital currencies and outside of it. He is not concerned with numbers, and it is apparent from his actions and lifestyle.

Zhao tried to domicile his company in China but had to quickly flee the country after the government enacted strict anti-crypto laws.

After moving around, he recently settled in Dubai and chose to live in a modest apartment and drive a Toyota minivan. He is also often spotted in simple attire donning black Binance-branded shirts.

Amy Winehouse had a lucrative career as a recording artist. She was wildly talented and deserving of fame. Unfortunately, troubles and demons plagued her. During her brief career, she made millions of dollars and started her own record label. Despite this, she was still miserable, and her drug addiction escalated. All she wanted was simple life as a singer. Money meant nothing to her, which was clear by her modest lifestyle.

Another example is the singer Natalie Imbruglia who was known as successful, rich, and unhappy. Natalie skyrocketed to fame in 1997 with the hit single "Torn". Scott Cutler and Anne Preven wrote "Torn" in 1993 with producer Phil Thornalley as a solo song for Preven. Cutler and Preven's band Ednaswap performed it live but did not initially release a recording. Ednaswap released a recorded version in 1995.

However, Imbruglia struck pay dirt with her recording, was hung around for fame and money, and then disappeared for a period. She claimed to have gone into seclusion after the one hit because the money and fame also brought unwanted people. Today she lives a less public life as a musician knowing that money is not what she needs.

Keanu Reeves has been in countless successful films such as Dangerous Liaisons, Bill & Ted's Excellent Adventures, Speed, Devil's Advocate, Matrix, John Wick, and one of my personal favorites, Something's Gotta Give. When he arrived in Hollywood, he realized partying, fame, and fortune were nothing in the big picture of life. He experienced very sobering moments with the loss of his best friend, River Phoenix, who famously overdosed in the Viper room. He also lost his pregnant fiancé in a car accident in the early 1990s.

Keanu knows the pains of life and is still vocal about living life. He talks about not needing money because it really does not dictate one's true happiness. That mindset allows him to make remarkable selfless gestures, such as giving his entire Matrix salary away because he has no emotional attachment to money. Have you seen him on YouTube giving away his seat on a subway train in New York to a woman? Acts of kindness are what bring happiness, not money.

Billionaires like Warren Buffett knows better from their struggles the value of money and life. He is the Chairman and CEO of Berkshire Hathaway and the third richest man on the planet. He believes in simple living and high thinking.

Facts about Warren confirm his beliefs about money. He has lived in the same house since 1958 that he bought for $31,500, invests in used cars instead of new vehicles, and prefers an economical breakfast such as McDonald's on his way to work. And, when he travels, he packs Oreo Cookies.

Warren does not believe in expensive mobile phones. His advice, consider your requirements and then buy a phone as per your feasibility. Moreover, you can save by choosing economical plans on calls and data.

Indulging in less expensive hobbies and minimizing buying designer goods are also wise. He plays the game bridge for about 12 hours a week, and during his free space, he loves playing ukulele and singing. He also carries the same wallet for the past twenty years.

Buffett believes in treasuring friendship, and longtime billionaire friend Bill Gates says their friendship is still strong because Warren goes out of the way to make people feel great about themselves. It is his lively and joyous attitude that makes him a thoughtful and kind friend.

Buffett believes in touching people's lives and emotionally connecting with them, which need not be expensive. For example, whenever Gates is in town, Buffett personally picks him up at the airport and often sends emails that he thinks the Gates family would love. Such special touches have helped him earn devoted friends in life, and people aspiring to live the Warren Buffett lifestyle must certainly take note of it.

Warren prioritizes relationships over material things and has said that no one can buy either health or love. That is why instead of playing golf on the fanciest golf course across the world, he loves to play golf in his city with the people he cares about. Making people envious of his belongings is not his goal.

Next on the list is luck. Have you got it? Ever heard or read something where they talk about luck being more important than intelligence? I would rather be lucky than smart. Are you familiar with the following proverb:

> *"You don't need intelligence to have luck, but you do need luck to have intelligence."*

Is this true? First, you need to believe in luck. According to Webster's dictionary, luck is a force that brings good fortune or adversity. A force? Are they talking about physics? Is it an electric, magnet electromagnet, or quantum force we are imaging? Is it something that holds quarks together like gluons, our bodies, or the planets?

Well, according to physicists, there is no definable force whatsoever associated with luck. According to them, the idea is frankly absurd. Even Webster defines a force as a strength or energy exerted or brought to bear: cause of motion or change: active power. You see, factually, luck does not exist! It is merely a human construct.

Here is a succinct example of reading about something such as luck that is false. And it is commonplace yet still passed along. You still read about luck frequently and use the word yourself more often than you are aware. How do these types of falsehoods affect your thoughts, actions, and even life's outcome?

Getting an education will set you up for success! I am going to take the heat on this one. Educators are not going to like seeing the following in print, but you should seriously consider the veracity of the statement.

Highly educated people all too often do not achieve their potential or success. There is no evidence that even suggests that highly educated people are more successful.

There is evidence that having a college degree has its benefits. According to data from the Bureau of Labor Statistics (BLS), the following are the benefits of pursuing a degree:

1. People that are at least 25 years old in 2021 with a bachelor's degree had a total unemployment rate of 5.5%, and those with only a high school diploma had a rate of 9.0%.
2. Median weekly earnings for those with a bachelor's degree was $1,305, versus $781 for those with high school diplomas.
3. There is no guarantee that a degree will increase your income, but it is arguable that the degree may jumpstart your career and speed up career advancement.
4. You are also likely to be considered more prepared than individuals who do not have an educational background in that field if you join an industry where you have been working toward a credential that has a high perceived value for employers.

Yes, having a degree has its benefits, but it does not ensure success as you compete with others that have more experience. Research shows that when it comes to evaluating employees, employers prefer to choose the candidate with the experience to get the job done. Ninety-one percent of employers responding to NACE's *Job Outlook 2017* survey prefer that their candidates have work experience, and 65 percent of the total group say that they prefer their candidates to have relevant work experience. In fact, as recent as 2022, global surveys show that 90% of employers prefer to hire graduates based on real work experience rather than educational background.

Frequently mentioned reasons why highly educated people are no more successful include not taking risks, working jobs they do not like, having low self-esteem, and not pursuing what excites them.

Countless people have a fear of failing because, from an early age, they get conditioned to believe that failure is a terrible thing. They have a self-esteem issue that they will not succeed. "Play it safe, and you are sure to succeed." It is reiterated ad nauseam and offers no guarantee of success. I have news for you, even cautious people fail or never realize their dreams by playing it safe, yet people still follow this advice.

Now, how sad is that?

What if instead of hearing failing is a terrible thing, we hear failing is a wonderful opportunity? Because we learn more from our failures than we do from our successes. Who wants to repeat their failures? No one! So, why not start by taking risks and learning quickly from the failures to avoid them in the future and achieve success faster?

What do you hope to achieve taking a job you do not want? To be fair, it may serve a purpose to make sure you get your bills paid, or it is a stepping stone to the job you do want. There is nothing wrong with paying your dues or being responsible and keeping a roof over your head and food in your mouth. However, if it is not a stepping stone, then is it in your best interest to stay in that situation long-term? What could you hope to achieve?

Living in Los Angeles, everyone has heard that to start as an agent, you must start in the mailroom. We all have heard the story of the Super High-Power Talent Agent that has the biggest celebrities started by delivering the mail to everyone in the agency.

Yes, it is true. I know someone myself that started delivering the mail to pay his dues and become an agent. He made it to the top and is Uber successful in representing dozens of A-list celebrities. I can also tell you for every one of them, there are hundreds of people who did not make it past the mail room. However, there are others that have made it straight to an agent out of either law or business school. What does the ratio of hundreds of failures to one success out of the mailroom tell you compared to those that have higher education? No, starting in the mail room is not the only way to becoming a successful agent in Hollywood.

If you cannot relate to the story, I recommend you watch the movie, "Swimming with Sharks." It is a fantastic movie released in 1994 with Kevin Spacey, John Whaley, and Michelle Forbes. It is an entertaining comedy about someone chasing their dream, having their character and limits put to the test, and what happens along the way. Consider your tolerance level in the pursuit of happiness when achieving your dreams.

Low self-esteem can be problematic in achieving happiness and success in your life. And it is true regardless of your level of education. Case in point, I attended Law School in Los Angeles. During my time in school, I had the privilege to meet the smartest teacher in all my years of school. He received his education from both an Ivy League Undergraduate & Law School.

I say this because even though he taught a law school course, what he more importantly taught was the process of how to learn. I am not talking about asking you to read and recant what you read or how to research. I am talking about the process of understanding information, answering any questions you may have yourself, and keeping the results. He is a brilliant man and an artist in his own right.

However, even to this day, he suffers from low self-esteem that has limited his career, ability to grow personally, and level of success. You see, despite his brilliance, he is socially inept. Behind the podium in the classroom, he is a maestro. But the moment someone approaches him after class or in a hallway one-on-one, he gets uncomfortable, cowers nervously, and fumbles over his words. In fact, he cannot even make eye contact which makes any attempt to have a connection impossible which limits his ability to succeed. I would be willing to bet you know someone akin to the professor.

What is the number of people you know that achieved financial success pursuing something that did not excite them or at least enjoy? These are professionals that pursued a passionless career. However, on a personal level, they sacrificed opportunities for other experiences, missing life's greatest moments.

Reasons professionals sometimes do not achieve their dreams are the following:

1. Fear of failure.

Taking risks is viewed as a negative thing. Our society dislikes risk, and we often equate failure with weakness. But the risk is simply taking a chance. It does not mean that you are a bad person. It does not mean that you are stupid. It does not mean that you are a fraud. It does not mean you will fail.

A major psychological tool for overcoming fear is acceptance. By embracing the possibility that you will fail, you can gain the courage to try something new. This kind of positivity and critical thinking isn't common in our society. Instead, we tend to focus on the worst-case scenario: the idea that failure is our only possibility.

2. The pressure of perfection.

One of the top reasons highly educated people do not live up to their true potential is because they have set a goal and are pursuing it relentlessly.

Rather than taking risks and trying new things, they are sticklers for achieving their goals — even when they are not achieving them.

Instead of setting individualized goals, these people set them for everyone else. They decide their values and goals, but they expect others to reach these things too. It is easier to believe that an individual can reach their goals than it is to say, "No."

3. Fear of the unknown.

It is challenging to step outside of our comfort zones when we spend so much of our time doing what we already know we excel at doing. Our mental models are our greatest barriers to achieving our potential. Think about the last time you faced an unknown challenge.

Have you ever started a new business, tackled a new area of study, or tried something entirely new? If the answer is yes, congratulations! You have already made a tremendous amount of progress toward your goal.

I cannot help but ask: were you willing to fail? Research shows that people often avoid decisions that might fail. They often make more decisions in favor of averting failure than in favor of doing what they want. This is not just true for risky decisions.

4. The feeling of belonging.

Highly educated people are often so busy focusing on what they do not want that they forget about what they do want. This lack of focus can create a disconnect between their minds and hearts. And this can lead to self-defeating habits.

High-achieving and highly educated people often fall short of their goals. They often have a tough time letting go of the past. It is difficult to appreciate their blessings when they are so concerned with what they are missing.

Having a life partner creates stability in life. If this is true, then how do you explain the following:

Marriages are becoming less common: in most countries, the share of people getting married has fallen in recent decades.

- Across most countries, people marry later in life.

- Cohabitation – couples living together who are not married is becoming increasingly common.

- Single parenting is common and has increased in recent decades across the world.

- There has been a general upward trend in divorce rates globally since the 1970s.[3]

According to the United States National Center for Health Statistics, approximately 4-5 million people get married every year in the U.S. ... and almost 42-53% of those marriages eventually end in divorce.

Furthermore, recent data shows more countries with divorce rates significantly above 50% as follows: Belgium 71%, Portugal 68%, Hungary 67%, Czech Republic 66%, Spain 63%, Luxembourg 60%, Estonia 58%, Cuba 56%, France 55%, and the US 53%.

We learn everything from our five senses. How limiting is this?

Body organs produce human senses called the 'human sense organs,' which receive stimuli or changes in the internal or external atmosphere and interpret it to create a nerve pattern in the nervous system. From there, an 'impulse' is sent out for the body to 'experience' or 'feel' the stimuli and respond. The process is complex and deep and therefore classified as a human body system called the sensory system.

Aristotle (384 BC – 322 BC) was the first to try to list the human senses, and it consisted of the five basic human senses we all learned. Over time, four more senses were added to his list. Those four were eventually differentiated for a total of 21 or up to 33, depending on the opinion of different neurologists. The human senses most widely accepted and related to human sense organs are as follows:

Consider this?!

The Basic Human Senses

1. Ophthalmoception — (Eyes) Sight or visual perception
2. Audioception — (Ears) Hearing or auditory sensations
3. Gustaoception — (Tongue) Sense of taste
4. Tactioception — (Skin)
5. Olfacoception or Olfacception — (Nose) Sense of smell

The Four Internal Human Senses

- 1. Thermoception — (Skin) Lack or increase of heat (temperature)
- 2. Proprioception — (Body Parts) Awareness of body parts w/o visual input
- 3. Nociception — (Whole Body) Sensation of pain (skin, body organs)
- 4. Equilibrioception — (Whole Body) Sense of balance (determined by ear fluid)

Additional Human Senses

1. Kinesthetic Sense — (Whole Body) Sense of acceleration
2. Tactility — (Mostly the Skin) Perception of pressure
3. Cutaneous Reception — (Skin) Sense of skin vasodilation (like flushed skin)
4. Chemoreception — (Blood and Brain) Sensation of hunger, thirst, vomiting and suffocation
5. Stretch Reception — (Muscles, Joints, and Skin) Sense of gag reflex, gas distension and excretion
6. Synaesthesia — (Body Parts) A combination of senses (like smiling at someone's voice)

EXTRASENSORY PERCEPTION*

1. Sixth Sense   (Small Brain) Sense of intuition (gut feeling)
2. Premonition   (Paranormal) Subconscious sense of future events (usually danger)
3. Telepathy   (Paranormal) Auditory perception of a person's (near or far) thoughts
4. Precognition   (Paranormal) Visual perception of future events
5. Clairvoyance   (Paranormal) Visual perception of invisible objects or events
6. Clairaudience   (Paranormal) Auditory perception of the invisible

Extrasensory perceptions are controversial human senses and have little to no scientific evidence.

Importance of Senses in Human Life

A person with no 'sense' of self or the world would be someone in the grave or a coma. In other words, 'sense' is very vital for a human being, and it is the senses we have that differentiate the living from the unconscious and the dead. For a person to be alive or even to exist in a vegetable state, their mechanoreceptors and interoceptors would have functions. Apart from consciousness, the role of human senses includes:

- Motion
- Reaction
- Emotion
- Articulation
- Interpretation
- Comprehension
- Cognition
- Recognition

- Sensation
- Perception

The study of the human senses and the human sense organs is very vast, intricate, and intriguing. Each organ in the sensory system works differently and uses unique sensors. That is why the findings and reports on the human senses and sense organs are varied and argued. Every acclaimed neurologist has his/her method of classifying and naming the different senses in the human body, which makes it difficult to keep track of or mention all the known human senses around the world.[4]

How consequential is getting the number of senses wrong? Well, I am willing to bet that neither you nor I have lost any sleep as a result. However, is it wise to dismiss the thought? It is possible the influence affected not only us but countless others directly or indirectly.

Think about all the things we evaluate and produce based on the five senses that impact our lives. Right off the cuff, there are foods, beverages, housing, consumer goods, drugs, medical products, energy sources, and countless other things. It would be naïve to believe that you have been immune to miscalculations based on someone's senses. Undeniably, people have left this planet based on those calculations… Asbestos, The Ford Pinto, Chernobyl, DES (Diethylstilbestrol).

One specific example that flew under the radar for decades is Trans Fat. Eating trans-fat raises the level of LDL ("bad") cholesterol in the blood. Approximately 540,000 deaths annually can be attributed to the intake of industrially produced trans-fatty acids. High trans-fat intake increases the risk of death from any cause by 34%, coronary heart disease deaths by 28%, and coronary heart disease by 21%. This results from the effect on lipid levels: trans-fat increases LDL ("bad") cholesterol levels while lowering HDL ("good") cholesterol levels. Trans fat has no known health benefits.[5]

From a medical standpoint, the results can be even more devastating. In 2015, an FDA analysis indicated that medical tests may use faulty assumptions or deliver inaccurate results leading to incorrect diagnoses. The same year the Institute of Medicine published a report indicating that about one in twenty people that receive outpatient care are diagnosed incorrectly.

In other words, 5%.

Is it acceptable for one out of twenty people to suffer because others are cutting corners? How would you feel if you were that one person?

Simply put, as a society, we do not place enough emphasis on getting things right. However, you have a choice! You can investigate the things that are critical to your future work to make not enough importance is placed on fact-checking. We tend to be lazy, which does not serve us well. Placing your trust in others is one thing, but don't you owe it to yourself to get the best information to make the best decisions and get the best result?

We owe it to ourselves to be more diligent about information. We learn not only from real-life experiences daily but also from books. In the case of reading, it is a wonderful thing to do for pleasure and to gain knowledge.

However, not everything we read is correct. And you know it. If you do not believe me, then think about the times you have read something to be true, and then you ignored it and did the exact opposite with a negative result. Do not feel bad because we all do it. It is human nature to question and doubt things.

Have you encountered other things to be incorrect? Ever played the game telephone? It is a game we often learn as children where we sit in a circle and pass along a saying or message by whispering it into the person's ear next to us. When the last person gets the message, they say it aloud, and it is rarely, if ever, the same as the initial communication.

Next time someone tells you something you believe to be of value, consider their source or investigate its validity on your own. I promise you will be surprised to see why the game telephone is not simply for entertainment. It is invaluable for us to learn early on that there is something of immense importance.

As information gets passed along, it gets misinterpreted, diluted, and eventually false. That is why not everything we hear is correct, and sometimes what we read is incorrect!

SOS does not stand for "Save our Ship" or "Shit on a Shingle," as the US marines allegedly once described their food. They only use it because it is the easiest to transmit three dots, three dashes, and three dots.

Perhaps consider what I learned at an early age and continue to pass it on to the people dear to me:

> *"Believe nothing of what you hear and only half of what you read."*

As our experience shows, people, even with the best intentions, are misinformed because of the source they got the information from. The information they learned has also been diluted down to quite possibly nothing of value, like in the game telephone.

However, in reading, someone has taken the risk to publish the information with their name attached for others to see. They have skin in the game because they are putting their reputation on the line. Also, once the information is seen, there becomes an opportunity to challenge or correct it.

Most people think at least twice before they put things in writing. For this reason, there is a higher probability that the information has been checked for accuracy. That is why I give it a 50/50 chance of being correct.

We oftentimes rely upon what others tell us and get poor results because the things we rely upon prove to be false. The proliferation of insufficient and bad information continues as it did since the beginning of time. Whether the world is flat, Saddam Hussein possesses weapons of mass destruction, or Donald Trump won the 2020 election. Falsehoods continue to live.

We may not agree that half of what people learn growing up is false. However, we cannot deny that a substantial amount is false and that information is relevant to our lives. More specifically, how it affects how we feel, act, react and succeed. We owe it to ourselves to realize the truth.

The point of this chapter is to illustrate that we are constantly fed false information that produces false and even detrimental results. What if we just accept it as the fact that worthless information is everywhere, and we owe it to ourselves to discover the truth? We want to have more positive experiences and better outcomes.

Simply put, as a society, we do not place enough emphasis on getting things right. We live in a sea of false information. Candidly, we are lazy! And, at times, that laziness comes at a cost, death!

However, you have a choice! You can investigate the things that are critical to your future, whether it is your health or personal or business success.

Placing your trust in others is one thing, but don't you owe it to yourself to get the best information to make the best decisions and get the best result?

It is critical to have an open mind and face these facts if you want to have more positive experiences and improve your chances of success. Because mindset matters!

Chapter 2

At This Moment, You Lack the Awareness of Knowledge or Experience to Reach Your Goal Now!

"I can't get no satisfaction!"

—Mick Jagger-

At this moment, you lack the awareness of knowledge or experience to reach your goals now! Exceptional and exciting news, isn't it? Do you know why? If you do not, do not worry, you are not alone.

Take a moment to consider how affirming and potentially empowering, transformational, and life-changing the statement is. Use your usual practice to analyze the description.

If you do not have one, you may use one I learned years ago and still find indispensable. It does not require you to purchase anything, make a substantial time commitment, or learn something new. In fact, it is extremely basic and only requires simple steps. With minimal practice, you may effortlessly integrate it into your daily life.

You begin by clearing your racing mind. Why is this necessary? As it was explained to me, your mind is a like a suitcase. If I filled the suitcase with articles, you would have no room to move around or include things that may be of greater value. So, clear your mind of all distractions to create space. This new space will allow you to identify any further distractions to be addressed, process information with less effort, and accommodate the latest information of greater value.

For me, there are two primary distractions. These are unwanted sounds and visuals. To solve the sound issue, I simply move to a quiet place. Very often, I do not have this option. So alternatively, I pop in my earphones and listen to soft, calming music. You want the music at a level that is just sufficient to drown out any unwanted sounds but not overwhelming where it dominates your thought process.

Next, I address the visuals by simply closing my eyes to eliminate anything visual. The object is not to experience total darkness. Rather, the idea is to get rid of visuals that are distracting, such as things that are moving. Eliminating the movement allows your eyes to rest and reduces the load on your brain.

Once you minimize the distractions, it is time to elevate the experience. You may incorporate breathwork to relax your mind. It can be as simple as a half dozen-controlled breaths in and out or more technical rhythmic breathing. The choice is yours, and I can tell you that with practice, the entire process becomes effortless, so do not get overly concerned. The most important thing is to get started.

After clearing your mind, is to ask a single question and wait. Here is where you will experience the most difficult challenge at first. Your mind will tend to wander. So, to counterbalance the wandering, stay focused on maintaining a steady and even breathing.

As you master the breathing, you will eventually lose awareness of your breathing. It is here where you will begin to receive new thoughts on the matter from a new perspective and a better solution.

Importantly, do not expect the technique to work the first time you try it. Like any skill, it needs to be developed. However, I can tell you from experience you can master it expeditiously and find the experience beneficial and rewarding.

Now back to the task of analyzing the statement. At this moment, you lack the awareness of knowledge or experience to reach your goals now! Considering asking yourself the following as part of your analysis:

1. What key elements do you notice?
2. What is the number of those elements?
3. What is their significance?

If you now have a clear mind, you should be able to see that we are dealing with time, awareness, information, experience, and goals. Five elements in total. Now think of the significance in terms of a mathematical equation to solve for an unknown variable. Let us attribute a letter to each of these elements as follows: Time (T), Awareness (A), Information (I), Experience (E), and Goal (G).

Your Goal is the ultimate thing to achieve. Therefore, it is the same as the product. In other words, if we total everything up, we should reach our Goal (G). Expressing our scenario in mathematical terms to solve for the Unknown would look as follows:

$$\text{Time (T)} + \text{Awareness (A)} + \text{Information (I)} + \text{Experience (E)} = \text{Goals (G)}$$

$$T + A + I + E = G$$

Now, here is where it gets interesting. You are the one who sets the Goal (G). Therefore, you already know the product. Time (T) is a human construct; it simply exists or not, depending on your scientific understanding. Either way, it is considered a Constant or neutral. And Information (I) and Experience (E) already exist.

Wait, did I read that correctly? Do information and Experience already exist?!

Correct, you can only absorb something that already exists. Case in point, consider a sponge that may absorb gas or liquid. For the sponge to absorb gas or liquid, it must already exist. Similarly, the brain may absorb Information and Experience only if they already exist. And Knowledge results from having Information and Experience, so you need not be concerned about it for this discussion.

I know it may be a difficult concept to accept or even consider that Information and Experience already exist. However, I ask you to table the matter of Information and Experience for now. I will address them later in the book.

I promise if you do not get fixated on this point, it will be well worth your while, even if you agree or disagree at that junction. Either way, you will still gain valuable information that will unlock new opportunities.

Back to our equation, it now would look like this:

$$T \text{ (Constant)} + A \text{ (Unknown)} + I \text{ (known)} + E \text{ (known)} = G \text{ (known)}$$

Or

$$A \text{ (Unknown)} = T \text{ (Constant)} + I \text{ (Known)} + E \text{ (Known)} + G \text{ (Known)}$$

The remaining variable is Awareness (A). Now think about it, if you only have one variable and can gain, or already possess, the requisite Awareness (A), you can solve the equation or your problem. In other words, you have what you need to achieve your goal. Because we know from mathematics you can solve any problem when there is only one remaining variable.

Now, in the context of the previous analysis, re-consider the statement: At this moment, you lack the awareness of knowledge or experience to reach your goal now! What is so powerful about the statement?

First, a problem needs to be solved. And, of course, recognizing something needs to be solved is critical. It means you are aware of the problem, and action needs to be taken if you want to solve it. Are you ready to act?

Second, looking at a frequent problem from a mathematical perspective can reduce the complexity of a problem. As you can see, in our example, only one variable needs to be solved. Sometimes, it is the case that you only lack one thing: Awareness (A). Do you feel more confident you can achieve your goal, knowing you only need to solve one thing?

Congratulations, you are now aware of what you need. Hopefully, you will take the necessary action to reach your goal. It will require additional learning, which requires an open mind. And, with an open mind, you will absorb the Information or Experience already in existence for you to achieve your goal.

If what I am telling you is true, would it potentially be transformational and life-changing? Think of all the things you may now achieve. Do you feel empowered?

Chapter 3

You Do Not Create Anything.

"We do not create the work; I believe, in fact, we are discoverers."

—Glen Murcutt-

To begin, I offer my deepest and sincerest apologies to all creators! Saying, "you do not create anything," is not meant to diminish anyone's valuable contribution to society or to discredit them. It is penned with the best intentions to illuminate another perspective, one that will serve you better.

Hopefully, for all the wonderful and visionary creators, we will soon credit them with a more worthy title. A title that truly captures the essence of their ability. One that is also self-empowering, illuminating, and encouraging to both the creator and others. It is long overdue!

My intention in this chapter is to provide clarity on the topic of creation to shift your mindset for the better. In other words, as we discussed in the previous chapter, things we learn are false. The idea that we create things is another one of those falsehoods. A falsehood that does not benefit you may impede you or even discourages you from attempting to achieve a goal.

Not everyone sees themselves as a creator or possessing the skill to create. Not all inventors and entrepreneurs think of themselves as creators. They believe they have an innate sense to pursue a path that feels more natural, comfortable, and aligned with their personality.

However, others who aspire to be inventors or entrepreneurs may have a distinct perspective. They may wonder and doubt if they have the requisite skill of a creator. It sparks uncertainty which does not improve your chances of success!

The next few pages to follow are meant for clarity. It may feel like a matter of semantics, which is fine. However, it is imperative to have clarity because words matter! The words lead to your behavior, your habits, your values, and your goals.

With that said, let us clarify the issue of creating and then move on to the more illuminating concepts. Concepts that may shift your perspective. They will hopefully open the door to new opportunities and possibilities. The kind that is genuinely realistic, more easily achievable, and life-changing.

Merriam Webster defines Create as to bring into existence or to produce or bring about by a course of action or behavior. Dictionary.com defines Create as to cause to come into being, as something unique that would not naturally evolve or that is not made by ordinary processes or to evolve from one's own thought or imagination, as a work of art or an invention. And other dictionaries have similar definitions.

Additionally, it is equally important to define imagination since it is part of the creation process. Dictionaries define imagination as the act or power of forming a mental image of something, not present to the senses or never perceived, and we define reality as the quality or state of being real.

According to the definition, to create something, you must bring it into being or existence. It would require information! And as I stated in the previous chapter, information already exists. It may be in a physical form or non-physical form, such as a thought, but nevertheless, it exists somewhere and in a form.

Whether it is an inventor or a theorist, they both imagine or visualize a product or theory and bring it to human existence. Even theories that do not exist, as we know them, do not mean they do not exist in the human realm or beyond the human realm in a form.

If this all sounds like a bunch of mumbo-jumbo, then stop reading here. I know it may seem hard to believe. Nevertheless, if you are still skeptical, then stop here, so I do not waste any more of your time.

However, keep in mind that what I am sharing with you is backed up by the most respected scholars, professors, and scientific experts of our time. It is not merely their opinions. It is validated by scientific formulas, which also happen to conform with the most established theories in human history.

My last disclaimer to you is the concepts that follow are controversial, even radical, and hard to grasp. However, as I said, they have the respect and support of the scientific community at large. These concepts are also responsible for providing a unique perspective fostering scientific research in areas otherwise ignored. The research is groundbreaking, monumental, disruptive, and responsible for unimaginable advancements in science. Come along if you dare!

We are now going to dive deeper further into the topic of creation by first examining the concept of time. Time is NOT real! It is a human construct. Humans use it to help differentiate between now and their perception of the past and future. It is an illusion made up of memories of everything that has ever been or ever will be happening now. And physicists can now show that everything happens at the same time.

Physicists, such as Max Tegmark of the Massachusetts Institute of Technology (MIT), explain that there is a block universe where time and space are connected, otherwise known as space-time. This theory conforms with Albert Einstein's theory of relativity that states space and time are part of a four-dimensional structure where everything thing that has happened has its own coordinates in space-time.

It allows everything to exist because the past, and even the future, are still there in space-time, making everything equally important as the present moment.

According to Tegmark, we can portray our reality as either a three-dimensional place where stuff happens over time or as a four-dimensional place where nothing happens ['block universe'] — and if it really is the second picture, then change really is an illusion, because there's nothing that's changing; it's all just there — past, present, future.

"We have the illusion, at any given moment, that the past already happened, and the future doesn't yet exist, and those things are changing."

"But all I am ever aware of is my brain state right now. The only reason I feel like I have a past is that my brain contains memories."

Julian Barbour, a British physicist who has authored books about time, describes everything as a series of "nows."

Dr. Barbour told physicist and author Adam Frank in the book 'About Time: Cosmology and Culture at the Twilight of the Big Bang': "As we live, we seem to move through a succession of Nows, and the question is, what are they?"

He explains, adding to the spacetime theory where everything has its own place: "You can think of it as a landscape or country. Each point in this country is a Now, and I call the country Platonia because it is timeless and created by perfect mathematical rules."

He adds that what we perceive as the past is simply an illusion formed in our brains.

Dr. Barbour: "The only evidence you have of last week is your memory. But memory comes from a stable structure of neurons in your brain now."

"The only evidence we have of the Earth's past is rocks and fossils. But these are just stable structures in the form of an arrangement of minerals we examine in the present."

"The point is all we have are these records, and you only have them in this Now."

Our birth, death, and every moment of our life are out there, somewhere, in space-time.

That is the Block Universe Model of our world.

In the block universe, time does not pass.

It often seems as though where we are "today" is present, "yesterday" is past, and "tomorrow" is future.

It also seems the present moment changes too — after all, tomorrow it will seem as though tomorrow is present, and yesterday it appeared yesterday was present!

So, from our perspective, time flows or passes. But in the block universe model, time does not flow.

In other words, in a block universe, there is no specific present moment, and "past" and "future" moments are relative.

Think about the idea of "here." I am here. You, while reading this, can honestly say, "I am here," even though your "here" is different from mine.

What is time?

On the block universe model, talking about the "present" or "now" works just like talking about "here."

Remember last week when you said to your friend, who was late arriving for coffee, "now you're here"; or when, long ago, Caesar said, "I am now crossing the Rubicon"?

These claims are both accurate. That is because all it means to talk about the present, or now, is to talk about the place in time where you are.

Since we are always located wherever we are (that is trivially true), everyone is in the present, just as everyone is located at the place they call "here."

According to the block universe view, time or temporal relations of "earlier than" and "later than" exist. These relations hold regardless of where anyone is located.

So, supposed Bert the dinosaur is located earlier than Sally the dog. That relation between Bert and Sally holds, regardless of whether we are located earlier than Bert or later than Sally.

Bearing this in mind, it is possible to see how to make sense of the idea of the past and future. Just as on this model, "now" picks out whatever time I happen to be located at, "past" picks out any time (or events at those times) that are earlier than my location, and "future" picks out any times or events that are later than my location.[6]

Now consider this. If everything already exists in our Block Universe, we do not create anything because it already exists. It is like a puzzle. It precedes the pieces it is cut into for someone to reassemble later. How fantastic is that?

Think about what I am about to tell you. Everything we humans have brought into existence is from things that already existed. Whether it is the wheel, theories, the airplane, the internet, or even thoughts, they have already existed, and we used what was available to bring them to fruition.

Consider this?!

Sound crazy? I do not think so. I challenge you to name one thing that came from something that did not previously exist because you cannot!

It may seem scary or unsettling. However, you should feel relieved and excited. Now you no longer need to spend time worrying if you can create something. Because if you can imagine it, it is because the thoughts and materials already exist. All you need to do is find the pieces, assemble them, and bring your thought to life just like Thomas Edison did with a better version of the light bulb to produce light.

If you were taught about the Block Universe when you were young, do you think you would have spent less time worrying about what you could accomplish? Would you have utilized that time to do other things and have other experiences? Would your existence be any different than it is?

According to the Block Universe Model, the reality you experience is what exists and what you are meant to experience. However, with better knowledge and access to information and experiences, you would experience a different reality. It is akin to taking a fork in the road and choosing one direction instead of another. Your destination may be different, or at the very least, the experience along the way is different.

Consider the idea I am sharing with you as something of value. Is it powerful, enlightening, and even transformational? Is it the information you have been looking for to transform and realize your dreams?

Now, consider this!? I am wrong, and you are right. The past, present, and future do not exist simultaneously. Congratulations, now you have a bunch of alternative scenarios to flood your mind and distract you.

For example, consider part of you believes that the information you seek does not exist. Alternatively, you may never experience the lessons needed to achieve your goals.

These are examples, and realistically, the possibilities are endless. Your chances now of focusing and finding the information and experiences you seek are low.

The truth? Either way, you need to find the information or experiences to achieve your objectives. Objectively speaking, which belief system do you feel will keep you more focused, efficient, motivated, and determined? Block Universe Theory, of course!

Chapter 4

If We Only Retain 20%, Or Less, Of What We Learn, Then Why Spend Time Reading and Memorizing Facts & Figures?

"It's easy to get trapped in a sticky web!"

—Spider Lockhart

I Before E Except After C, 3.14159265358979323846, Plymouth Rock, $a^2 + b^2 = c^2$, Gliese 581d, Fourscore and seven years ago...

Can you tell me the significance of each of the following references:

I Before E Except After C. A ridiculous rule. Perhaps more so to me because my first name, Keith, is an exception to the rule. No one could ever explain to me why my name was an exception other than it was because I am special. When I was young, I found it more frustrating than flattering. Look how many other exceptions there are:

- When sounded as "AY," as in neighbor and weigh.
- When sounded as "EYE," as in Einstein.

Many words are commonly thought of as being exceptions. However, they are spelled correctly. There is no easy way to remember these words. The list of commonly mistaken words is below:

Neither, weird, foreign, leisure, seize, forfeit, height, protein, caffeine, forfeiture, codeine, and heifer.

CIEN words, for example:
- Efficient
- Ancient
- Conscience
- Sufficient

Is it me? Am I crazy thinking memorizing all of this is a waste?

The number 3.14159265359 is Pi or the mathematical ratio of the circumference of a circle to its diameter. Very cool to remember the number and as many decimal numbers as possible as a kid. But why be encouraged to do so?

Why not just remember that Pi is the solution to solving the variable of the diameter or circumference of the circle? Instead, we are encouraged and even asked to memorize the whole number and a bunch more digits. As my first physics professor, Mr. Logan, would say, "it is all esoteric," and it is taking up unnecessary space in our brains.

How about Plymouth Rock? It is hard to imagine that anyone would place such tremendous significance on such a small object, originally 10 tons or roughly 30' x 6'. It is not an object you would notice from the sea and navigate towards. In other words, it's no Rock of Gibraltar. However, this rock is world famous, with more than a million visitors each year.

Plymouth Rock is the traditional site of disembarkation of William Bradford and the Mayflower Pilgrims , who founded Plymouth Colony in December 1620. The Pilgrims did not refer to Plymouth Rock in any of their writings; the first known written reference to the rock dates back to 1715 when it got attention in the town boundary records as "a great rock." The first documented claim that Old Thomas Faunce made the first documented claim that Plymouth Rock was the landing place of the Pilgrims in 1741, 121 years after the Pilgrims arrived in Plymouth.[7]

I will leave the math to you and its significance. Do you believe it's worth memorizing and the stories associated with it?

Who loves Pythagoras? I bet you do not even know who he is! Pythagoras is credited with, among other things, figuring out how to calculate the unknown length of a side of a triangle. His famous formula $a^2 + b^2 = c^2$ is taught, to this day, in schools around the world. We still ask students to memorize it.

Gliese 581g - After years of saying habitable exoplanets are just around the corner, planet hunters found one in 2018. Gliese 581g is the first planet found to lie squarely in its star's habitable zone, where the conditions are right for liquid water. An absolutely exciting discovery! There are most likely more than 100 billion stars and planets in our Milky Galaxy. Yet, Gliese is getting all the attention because it is within the small sector that we chose to survey in the night sky. Is it worth memorizing?

"Four score and seven years ago, …." is one of the most famous speeches and YES, still taught in school to this day. Yet, even those of us that remember parts of the speech forget that a four score is equal to 80 years.

So, what is the point of all of this? As Mr. Logan would say, "it is all esoteric." In other words, information that is only known by a few and most likely not worth remembering!

These are a handful of examples of information we are encouraged to retain that have little value in the overall scope of our lives. Are educators genuinely interested in us memorizing and retaining "fun facts?" Perhaps they see these experiences as memory exercises to expand our memory.

In addition to memorizing fun facts, we also learn through experiences. Notably, experiences occur with significantly greater frequency than memorizing facts. And they happen whether we want them or not. We also misinterpret them, and they prove to be false over time.

Have you ever burned your finger on a stove? How about your arm in the oven? Weren't you ever warned by someone to be aware and careful of these situations? We can agree this is essential information, yet most people still have the unpleasant experience of being burned by a stove or oven more than once.

So, why did it happen? Did you think the information was unimportant or false, or you forgot? How many times did it take for you to learn this lesson? The point is that even basic everyday life lessons are not so easy to retain.

How about grocery shopping? Have you already memorized all the items in your favorite store, so you need not walk all the aisles for future visits? Of course not, because we know from experience that products change and sometimes move. Therefore, memorizing them and where they are is not the best use of our time.

Research shows that birds and humans have different networks of neurons in their brains. Nevertheless, their working memory is limited by similar mechanisms.

Working memory is the brain's ability to process information for a short time in a retrievable state. It is essential for performing complex cognitive tasks, such as thinking, planning, following instructions, or solving problems. A team of researchers from Ruhr-Universität Bochum (RUB) has now succeeded in investigating this special area of memory in birds in more detail and in comparing it to data storage in the mammalian brain. The scientists found that birds and monkeys -- despite their different brain architecture -- share identical central mechanisms and limits of working memory.

The researchers from the Neural Basis of Learning department at RUB published the results in the journal eLife on 3 December 2021.

The capacity of working memory is limited. Humans can only take in about four items of information simultaneously -- and it was precisely this limitation that made the Bochum researchers curious. "There are various theories about how limitation occurs in the brain and what role the network of neurons plays in this," describes first author Lukas Hahn. "However, the existing models are based exclusively on studies in humans and other primates. We wanted to complement these with our expertise."

Hahn, who works at the Faculty of Psychology in the department of Professor Jonas Rose, specializes in researching the neuronal basis of cognition in the avian brain. "The working memory of some birds, such as crows, has a capacity similar to that of humans, although their brain architecture is very different from that of mammals," says Jonas Rose, head of the Neural Basis of Learning department at RUB. "We wanted to know: How can brains with such clear structural differences produce working memories with similar capacities?"

To do this, the Bochum scientists observed crows at the Faculty of Psychology in Bochum. They assessed the birds' working memory with an exercise originally developed for macaque monkeys. "We taught the crows to look at a screen and memorize a different number of colored squares there," explains Hahn. "After a pause with one second of black screen, we presented them the squares on the screen again, but slightly different. The birds were now tasked with figuring out which square had changed."

While the crows performed the task, the scientists recorded neuron activity in an area of the brain corresponding to the prefrontal cortex -- the central hub of cognition in mammals. "The studies showed that the neurons in the crows' brains responded to the changing colors in virtually the same way as the neurons in monkeys," analyses Rose. Moreover, the scientists noticed that increasing the number of items the crows had to remember altered the amount of information individual neurons encoded to the same degree that had been previously observed in monkeys.

Lukas Hahn: "The similarities between the distantly related bird and mammalian species confirm pre-existing core ideas about the limits of working memory. Moreover, they suggest that birds and apes share the same core mechanisms and limits of working memory despite their different brain architecture." And Hahn already has ideas for a follow-up project in mind, namely investigating how different regions of the birds' brains process working memory signals with each other. "That would be an exciting future question to uncover more neural bases of cognition in the avian brain."[8]

Do you consume countless books? Have you read hundreds, thousands, or more articles? How about labels? Can you quantify the amount of information you have viewed or even captured from the internet?

Now, what about experiences? Can you recall them all, half, a fraction? Or better yet, mention the number of lessons you have learned.

Frankly, in the best of any of these cases, it is infinitesimal in relation to all that exists, and I will tell you why.

According to Forrest Wickman, computational neuroscientists generally believe the brain stores 10-100 terabytes of data. For comparison, most laptops store 8 to 16 gigabytes of information. Using 16 gigabytes, the brain can store .016 terabytes. In other words, your brain can store at least 625 times more information than your laptop. Quite impressive![9]

If it all seems confusing, the chart below should help you.

METRIC	VALUE	BYTES
BYTE (B)	1	1
KILOBYTE (KB)	$1,024^1$	1.024
MEGABYTE (MB)	$1,024^2$	1.048.576
GIGABYTE (GB)	$1,024^3$	1.073.741.824
TERABYTE (TB)	$1,024^4$	1.099.511.627.776
PETABYTE (PB)	$1,024^5$	1.125.899.906.842.624
EXABYTE (EB)	$1,024^6$	1.152.921.504.606.846.976
ZETTABYTE (ZB)	$1,024^7$	1.180.591.620.717.411.303.424
YOTTABYTE (YB)	$1,024^8$	1.208.925.819.614.629.174.706.176

The amount of estimated data in the world in 2020 was 44 zettabytes. And by 2025, the amount of data generated each day is expected to reach 463 exabytes globally. Google, Facebook, Microsoft, and Amazon store at least 1,200 petabytes of information.

Those 44 zettabytes are equivalent to 44,000,000,000 terabytes, and remember, your brain can only retain somewhere between 10-100 terabytes. In other words, we are all surrounded by a sea of information and experiences of which we will only encounter a tiny portion.

So, what is so important about this reality? As my grandfather once warned me, "choose wisely!" And that applies here to what we choose to remember of the infinite information and experiences.

I am sure you will agree from the 30,000-foot view that the amount of information and experiences that exist is overwhelming.

So, rather than attempting to memorize a maximum amount of knowledge, a better strategy is to learn how to access it when you need it. A good analogy is what I learned from a brilliant Harvard-educated law professor in my first semester of law school. "Do not bother to learn the law!" The law is dynamic. It changes, evolves, meanders, and does so frequently.

Interesting? I thought to myself for a moment... less work for me. Sounds good! And wow, it turned out to be great advice not only for the law but for everything else in life. Do you think I am kidding? No, but let me explain.

The reasoning behind the Harvard professor's comment is abnormally simple. The law is not stagnant. It is constantly changing. We can see it to be true in the recent court decision to overturn the famous case of Roe v. Wade. Pouf, just like that, fifty years of precedent gone in an instant.

Fortunately, the good old professor was nice enough to elaborate. He shared that all that is important is to know how to get the information when you need it. At the time of this conversation, he was referring to the law library stacked with fancy hardcovered books. Those books were eerily, dark in color with gold engraving and weighed about five pounds each.

That conversation was about thirty-five years ago. Today, I am sure the same law library looks quite different. Absent of books, I imagine with all the information now in digital format and accessible in a fraction of time on a computer.

Although, I am willing to bet the filing format is no different and akin to the Dewey Decimal System. Remember good old Melvil Dewy, the man responsible for that proprietary library classification system allowing new books to be added to a library in their appropriate location based on the subject? Yes, all the way back to 1876 in the United States and another one of those fun facts taking up valuable RAM, random access memory in your brain.

There have been so many advances in cataloging and accessing information in recent years. It is truly remarkable how computers have transformed our lives. There are also lesser-known discoveries and advancements that are about to transform our lives.

Consider this?!

As I mentioned previously, in one of the earlier chapters, information and experiences already exist. Yes, they do, and here is where you will get to see how and where.

Does it still sound too good to be true? It did to me at first. It was not until I learned more about other theories of science that were confirmed that I decided to accept these things as facts. After all, it is difficult to argue with scientific theories once they are validated and conform with other well-established laws within the sciences.

Before we dive straight into how and where information and experiences exist, we must first take a closer look at the human brain. There are many things we still do not know about the brain. However, there is also an astounding amount that we do know. Understanding the brain will set the stage for you to potentially unlock one of the greatest gifts you will ever receive.

Our brains are made of thousands of neurons, or brain cells, and contain many different structures. But the cerebral cortex envelopes all of them.

This 'cortex' is the outermost layer of the brain and is responsible for complicated cognitive functions like thinking, reasoning, memory, personality traits, and language.

The deeper parts of the brain take care of the more 'primitive' aspects of our lives, such as fears, impulses, subconscious, and emotions.

Our brains also have another layer, known as the subcortex, that forms a direct connection to the cortex and plays a vital role in processing and transmitting data.

After briefly going over the brain's biology, it's time to talk about one of its most vital functions: memory. After all, what's the point of processing new information if you can't store it?

Memory is an automatic process, which is why we normally pay too much attention to it.

Each event, whether big or small, passes through our brain's memory centers, whether we realize it or not. However, most of the information passing through is not stored permanently.

There are three types of memory.

Sensory memory

When our brains are triggered by an external sensory stimulus, it briefly retains the information after the original stimulus fades away.

For instance, if you've watched sparklers lit or car lights in traffic at night, you must have noticed that the light seems to leave behind a trail before vanishing. This is due to 'iconic memory,' the visual type of sensory memory.

Even though the stimulus no longer exists at the moment, our brain still stores its impression for a short time. The mind then has the option to either forget this information or process it further through the brain's 'memory banks.'

The other two types of sensory memory include echoic (auditory) memory and haptic (tactile) memory.

An important thing to note is that unlike short and long-term memory (more on that later), sensory memory is not consciously controlled. The main role of sensory memory is to create a detailed and complete representation of our sensory experience.

In learning, sensory memory can be triggered by using elements that stimulate the senses, such as background music or visual images in presentations.

Short-term memory

Short-term memory, also known as working memory, allows for the temporary storage of information when triggered by a stimulus.

According to experts, this type of memory can retain only about seven items. On top of that, it also has a short time limit of about 10-60 seconds.

Long-term memory

After going through short-term memory channels, relevant information advances to long-term stores.

At this point, our brains are far less likely to forget important information. But even this type of memory can decline if relevant details are not recalled.

Although there are various theories regarding how information gets processed in the brain, most experts agree that the process involves three crucial stages:

- Input. In the first stage, the mind is triggered by a stimulus, in response to which it evaluates and analyzes the captured information. It is in this stage that the brain decides whether the information is worth remembering or not.
- Storage. In the storage stage, the brain organizes, encodes, and stores the information for future use. However, the brain may forget the information stored over time if it's not reinforced.
- Output. During this last stage, the brain determines the best way to use this information and how it should respond to the stimulus. For instance, after reading a set of instructions, your brain allows you to use the newly gained knowledge to complete a task.[10]

I find the human brain fascinating. As you were learning about how the brain works, did any of it sound familiar? Did it sound as if someone was describing a computer? Input? Processing? Transmitting? Memory? Storage? And so forth?

Where did the idea of a computer come from anyway? Did someone get the idea to replicate the brain? These are all valuable questions to ask! Because, with questions, answers will come.

Do you know when you are born, your brain comes pre-loaded with an operating system, information, and experiences? Analogous to when you purchase a new computer. You know what I mean. When you take it out of the box, it already has an operating system, programs, and a certain amount of information, experience, and memory waiting to be operational.

Now it is time to assess your memory. Did the previous explanation of the brain mention that all information and experience are already in your brain? We discussed functions like thinking, reasoning, memory, personality traits, and language. I think of these as the processor, RAM, hard drive, and programs pre-loaded on your new computer.

However, when it comes to information and experience, the passage discusses the onboarding of information and experience from stimuli. It also mentions the processing, and at times the storage, of that information and experience. I think of this as new information, experience, or pictures you add to your computer that fills up your hard drive.

You see, they are similar. The brain and a computer have a working short-term memory or RAM and long-term memory like a hard drive. They also both accept and process information and experience.

Consider this?!

So, where do the information and experience come from? Oops, I guess they must already exist. Did you know that information cannot be lost permanently? Even if you send knowledge to a black hole, which destroys everything, it will not destroy the knowledge.

Stephen Hawking once proposed that black holes will eventually evaporate due to Hawking radiation. Thus, all information eaten by the black hole is destroyed. However, this violates physics, and hawking soon recanted his views. I'm willing to bet the same is true of experience. Experience is the interaction and observation of facts or events that is information.

Spoiler alert! Information and experience are everywhere, and it doesn't get destroyed! Yes, it is true! Okay, so if it is true, then where is it? Well, thanks to modern-day science, we can answer that question. Any guesses? I'll give you a hint. We touched on it earlier.

It is in the Block Universe we occupy!

If you can believe that all information and experience already exist and your brain is capable of processing it, then perhaps all you need to do is learn how to capture and process it. Is such a thing even possible? Why would it not be conceivable?[11]

We can agree the human brain is the same as a computer. Meaning we have limited working and long-term memory, and then we can agree on the importance of choosing knowledge to retain. And, if you do not agree, that is perfectly fine. Because later in the book, I will offer you another alternative to consider. An alternative that may not only remove limitations but also gives you access to much greater possibilities.

Reading is also a wonderful opportunity to memorize or retain facts & figures. It gives the opportunity to hear and learn from other people's experiences. We are talking about potentially fast-tracking your way to solutions with less work, challenge, and heartache.

Do you believe we have an unlimited capacity to retain knowledge? Do computers? No!

The human brain has a limited capacity to retain information. However, we need not have the unlimited brain capacity to be successful. Believing we have limited brain capacity creates the opportunity to carefully choose essential information to retain or consider other options. Yes, memorizing and having faster access to that information saves time and quite possibly improves your chances of success. And, when you learn what is coming later in this book, it may not even be necessary to remember anything.

Chapter 5

You Spend A Disproportionate Amount Of Time Thinking How To Solve Problems Than Solving Problems.

"Give time some time, it will solve most of your problems."

—Lokesh Giri-

Henry Ford, the American Industrialist and Founder of the Ford Motor Company, had a similar thought when he said, "Most people spend more time and energy going around problems than in trying to solve them."

Albert Einstein said, "No problem can be solved from the same level of consciousness that created it." His words of enlightenment encourage people not to waste time attempting to solve problems at the same level of consciousness. Instead, take a distinct perspective to achieve a different level of consciousness to solve the problem.

A recent survey of more than 30 organizations reveal that employees spend an average of 3 hours per week solving work-related issues that could easily be solved if they had access to the proper support.

Management consulting firm Trenegy Incorporated conducted the study across a variety of industries, including healthcare, energy, manufacturing, distribution, and professional services. They asked, "On an average week, how much time do you spend trying to solve work-related problems or seek answers that could be quickly addressed by someone else in your company if you just knew who to contact?" Respondents ranged from new employees to executive leadership and everything in between.

Work-related issues were widespread, including problems with recent technology or software upgrades, HR and benefit questions, company policy questions, field support for technical problems, and issues with facilities.

As mentioned above, employees spend an average of *three hours* per week solving work-related issues that could easily be solved internally if employees only knew who to ask.

This means a typical 1,000-employee organization wastes $6MM a year on inefficient problem-solving. That is huge.

The study also revealed a significant correlation between the number of years of employment and the amount of time spent troubleshooting. Employees at the company for less than five years spent up to 15 hours per week troubleshooting, while the more tenured employees spent around one hour.

They also found out that the larger the organization, the more pervasive the problem. Organizations with the most employees reported the highest percentage of time spent trying to find the right support expert. Employees give up and simply hope they can find a satisfactory solution themselves.

Traditional means of problem-solving either result in 1) wasted hours trying to troubleshoot something alone or 2) the problem passed around the organization like a hot potato. Kara McCracken, Trenegy analyst, explains, "Most large organizations offer too many options for finding support, including emails, self-service portals, IT help desks, ticketing systems, and phone numbers. Making matters worse, these solutions are over-engineered and rarely provide a rapid response."

Lindsey Ligon, Trenegy analyst, adds, "As the number of millennials entering the workforce increases, the need for better problem-solving tools becomes more important."

Traditional enterprise service management (ESM) solutions have failed to truly address hours wasted on problem-solving. These ESM solutions rarely connect an employee to the right person the first time. Response time is often measured in days or weeks, and automated AI and self-service portals do not work.

Think about problems you have agonized over unnecessarily. Can you recall the turning point when you finally decided you needed to change your approach before you could act? It is most likely embarrassing.

Case in point, I was in a foreign country and needed my clothes cleaned. The first thought I had was to ask someone. However, my experience from the time I landed until the time I walked into my room was hopeless in terms of communication. Naturally, I felt helpless and terribly negative.

I sat on the bed and decided to try Google cleaners, but the search results were all in a foreign language, and the mapping option did not work. I thought for five minutes, and then it hit me. I decided to take inventory of my clean clothes and the days I could last until I was out of clean clothes. I realized I had two days left.

Now that I was aware that I was not out of time, I opted to focus on my work and other things. I had a commitment to keep me busy and still time remaining. I figured I would deal with it later.

The next day arrived, and the problem crossed my mind. I decided to walk the neighborhood. I will come across at least one place to clean my clothes.

I walked for four miles acquainting myself with the neighborhood, but there were no cleaners. I thought to myself, whatever, and decided I would deal with it tomorrow and headed back to the hotel.

Day two came, and I realized I was down to the last of my clean clothes. I had a few hours left to find a solution, yet still empty-handed. I needed to change my plane ticket, and it required my passport. I went to the safe to extract it, and low and behold, there was a laundry form and a thin plastic bag sitting on top of the safe.

I collected all the dirty clothes, threw them in the bag, and headed to the lobby with the bag in one hand and the laundry form in the other. The gentlemen behind the desk were present when I signed my room number on the form. I gave him a thumbs-up and walked away. The whole solution took me five minutes after spending hours of thought and action.

At 9:00 am, there was a knock on my door. I opened the door, and before me stood a woman with a big smile and my clothes in her hands. It was all quite simple, satisfying, and embarrassing. Can you relate?

How about deciding to end a relationship with someone? It can take days, weeks, months, or even years. Yet, once you decide to act, it is over in seconds, minutes, or hours.

Booking a trip or a hotel lately?

How about investing your money? We spend days and weeks evaluating investment opportunities. Once we decide, it takes a fraction of the time to execute a trade or a day or two to close a transaction.

The point of these comments is that efficient problem-solving requires an approach from a different level of consciousness than which it came about, a procedure, an action, or in other instances, deliberate inaction.

If you want to solve problems, it is imperative that you have a definable process. A process that you can explain to someone without having to refer to anything. If you cannot explain your process without referring to something to refresh your memory, then you do not have enough practice.

A lack of practice is much greater than a detail. There unquestionably will be times when you will not have the luxury of time. Not understanding your process can cost you an opportunity or even your life.

I have forty years of scuba diving experience. I have been trained to search, rescue, and save people above and below water. The reason I went through the training is because the number one cause of death for scuba divers is diver error, 60%. Divers that do not frequently dive often forget their training. It even holds for those that have the most training.

I had one diving experience that prompted me to get a Search and Rescue Certification. Astoundingly, I was in a situation and could have drowned…. and not by my own doing.

I was diving in underground caverns with three other divers. I had more than sufficient training and experience. They put me in between two divers with more experience because I had the least training. The diver in front of me got trapped on the ceiling above and could not deflate his buoyance compensator device (BCD). If you are not familiar with a BCD, it is a life jacket for divers that you can inflate and deflate to keep you balanced underwater.

The diver diligently tried to deflate his BCD by attempting to raise the hose above his head to dump his air. However, he could not because he was lying horizontally against the ceiling. He continued to try to push off the ceiling to create space, but he could not create enough space.

The divers in front of him were unaware of the situation, and the diver behind me could not pass me because we were in a narrow passage. The diver was reaching for me desperately, and the rules of diving were clear in my head.

Never dive alone. Your safety comes first. Never approach a panicked diver unless you have the proper training. The reason is panicked divers will grab you, unintentionally get you entangled, and render you both in a dangerous situation that often leads to both divers running out of air and drowning. Add the fact that we were in a cavern, not the open ocean, which made it even more dangerous.

I knew how to solve his problem, but I did not know how to approach him because he was now in a desperate panic. I sat in disbelief as I watched. I thought to myself, "this guy is going to drown in front of me, and I am going to have to push his dead body out of the cavern." The thought made me shudder and feel ill. Precious minutes continued to pass.

With little time left to spare, the diver in front of the panicked diver turned around. He saw the man in a frenzy and managed to turn himself around, swim back a considerable distance, and approach the panicked diver from behind. He pulled the emergency relief valve on the BCD, causing it to deflate the jacket.

Yes, it was as simple as that, pulling a short rip cord that we all learn about in case of an emergency. It took seconds to solve a problem the diver could not solve in minutes. However, the diver found himself in a situation he had never experienced and just forgot his training or the process of dumping air. It almost cost him his life.

Fortunately, everything turned out fine; no one died! However, the situation was traumatizing for everyone. We discussed the situation at length on the boat ride home and continued at a restaurant nearby for hours.

The whole time I felt like a remorseful "Good Samaritan" that intentionally failed to act. I was crawling in my skin because the panicked diver knew I was willing to let him die. I could not look at him or myself.

We eventually talked through all the details of the dive, a customary practice like a debriefing, and the other divers praised me for following my training. They said had I not, the situation could have been far worse. That day I signed up for the Search and Rescue Certification.

If you underestimate the seriousness of a problem or situation, you may be in for a shocking surprise. It happens to everyone. The question is: Are you prepared? Do you have a process you know well enough that you can rely on to get you the best result?

In my scuba diving incident, I was prepared and followed the process I learned. Likewise, the lead diver followed the process he learned to rescue someone and did exactly that without me complicating the matter.

I highly recommend you consider the disproportionate amount of time you spend thinking about how to solve problems and solving them. Seriously consider immediately adopting a problem-solving strategy. It does not have to be overkill but something to give you structure and practice. I would not want you to miss an opportunity!

Consider developing a problem-solving process. If you do not have one, I believe you will like one of the two that follow:

Next time you face a challenge, consider executing the following basic steps:

1. Do Not Judge What You Are Doing
2. Remain Detached and Objective
3. Identify the Problem
4. Turn the Problem into a Question
5. Describe the Problem
6. Analyze the Problem
7. Identify the Root Cause(s)
8. Develop The Easiest & Most Plausible Solution
9. Consider Alternative Perspectives
10. Develop Alternative Solutions
11. Execute

    - Implement a Solution
    - Measuring the Results
    - Adjust the Solution or Implement Another

Remember, if you want the best result, you will need to memorize the steps before you are presented with a challenge. I cannot stress this point enough. However, it is up to you.

I know it may seem intimidating but believe me, this is much better than memorizing "Fourscore and seven years ago…," Pi or who starred in "Gone with the Wind." Also, it is not that difficult to learn a process if you do it one step at a time and understand how each step is connected to the next. Do not allow yourself to be intimated by thought alone!

Alternatively, consider the following method for challenges with greater complexity. Such challenges require a deeper understanding and more work. Also, if you enjoy always delivering your "A-Game," you may prefer it.

The reason I am sharing more details is that I want you to be prepared for when the opportunity comes knocking. The following is meant for more of a group scenario, but there are things to glean from it, even if you choose to implement it yourself.

First off, you will need to identify the problem. It is typically the easiest element because it is apparent. However, there are situations where the situation is to the contrary.

Next, develop a problem statement that details the problem or position. Alternatively, you may pose the problem as a question that needs to be solved. People tend to prefer the second choice.

Next comes the tricky part, identifying a solution. Sometimes, it is difficult to see a solution to a complex problem. Engaging others can be extremely helpful in gaining different insights and perspectives. That assistance could lead to a much more efficient solution. Caution, be sure you have facts, if necessary, to back things up before executing the solution.

Importantly, develop alternative solutions before acting on your first option. Yes, you may need to tweak your original plan as you go or even implement another.

It is perfectly normal and acceptable to maintain your awareness, coolness, and objectivity if you want to save time.

Set up KPIs (key performance indicators) if possible.

Monitor what you are doing to gain valuable feedback. Remember, IF YOU CAN'T MEASURE IT, YOU CAN'T IMPROVE IT! With the feedback in hand, from your initial choice, you can make either stay the course, adjust, or pivot to plan B.

Also, do not forget to maintain objectivity. Do not get sucked into your emotions or biases. Being emotional or biased can derail you, especially when analyzing feedback and adjusting the plan. Doing so has a high probability of making things worse, and I mean fast!

Keep a written record of everything, also images if applicable. You will need it to reflect on your actions. Having the information handy will eliminate any doubts and save you considerable time trying to recall what you forgot.

If you are working in a group, designate a third party for further objectivity and resolve any conflicts between the members of the group. Also, create a roadmap that breakdowns the action plan and provides timing benchmarks for everyone's reference.

Next, seriously consider the constituents of the group. The more people you include and the more diverse, the more perspectives and viable solutions you will achieve. I am a huge proponent of diversity and inclusion and have been interviewed a dozen times on this topic.

There are times when solutions are temporary, and a more substantial solution is needed. To solve such a problem, you need to get the cause of the matter. For instance, it is analogous to a doctor giving you antacid pills to stop a burning sensation in your stomach when all you have is a bacterial infection that needs antibiotics. The antacid may treat the symptom, but it does not solve the real problem.

In these cases, it is best to ask all the questions that come to mind. I recommend resorting to the most obvious, who, what, where, when & why. These are compelling questions and especially in a group setting.

Think about it. Would you prefer visiting one doctor that decides to prescribe antacid pills or a group of doctors that share their knowledge? There is a much higher probability in the group they will recognize the infection and give the antibiotics the first time out instead of repeat visits to the same doctor.

Another technique is to give the group a brief time limit to solve the problem. Very often, people produce the best solutions under pressure. Ever heard the quote by Thomas Edison, "necessity is the mother of invention"?

Yes, people work better now that time is running out. It is an opportunity to get laser focused and draw upon all your resources.

How about appealing to the group with an incentive? Are you familiar with the saying the best man wins or the X-Prize? How about SpaceX? How do you think they took over Nasa's exclusive business of launching satellites? Simple, the government said, "hey Elon, if you can do it better and cheaper, the job is yours!" There is nothing like getting a reward and dopamine.

How about a round table or what we call today, a think tank? Get everyone in the same room, and no one leaves until the problem is solved. Being stuck in a room is enough motivation for anyone to solve even the most complex obstacle.

One of my favorite technics is SWOT Analysis. I learned about it from Magic Johnson years ago. People know Magic as a Laker and Basketball great. However, he is also a brilliant businessperson. I had the honor and pleasure of spending time with him and learning about business. You see, I never went to business school or studied any business in school. I studied biochemistry and used my math and analytic skills in business settings.

The SWOT Analysis is brilliant in its simplicity. You take a piece of paper if you are old school or on your computer, and you create four columns with the headings Strengths (S), Weaknesses (W), Opportunities (O), and Threats (T).

You then compile a list of attributes of the business or problem under each heading. Once you feel you have exhausted the attributes, you then focus on what you need to improve, solve, capitalize on, or protect.

It is a fun exercise. The more practice you get, the more proficient you become. You feel like you are playing a game, and when you capitalize on your efforts, you will feel gratified. If you adopt this technique, I can practically guarantee that you will eventually catch yourself doing it naturally. You will be presented with an opportunity to the problem and find yourself automatically categorizing your thoughts in these four columns.

Problem-solving can be simple, complicated, and even multifaceted. Utilizing the best techniques can simplify and expedite the process. Along the way, you will have the opportunity to develop methods to be used for future challenges.

Additionally, you may minimize stress, the anxiety that comes with acting, and the negative feelings associated with tasks. Consider the techniques and strategies you feel most comfortable with and get started today. Develop a process that will serve you well when you are faced with an opportunity or challenge.

Chapter 6

You Are Not In Flow!

"Do not go with the flow. Be the flow."

—Elif Shafak-

"Don't you know? I am in the flow!"

Wow, it sounds unbelievable! Doesn't it? I remember the first time I heard someone proclaim they were in the flow. She was a new acquaintance and viewed things from a unique perspective. Upon her orating those magic words, my eyes popped, and I felt a tingly sensation wave over me. I began to imagine being within a warm, cozy cocoon carried away by the forces of nature. Yes, it was enlightening, and my mind became flooded with questions.

"Claudia, what exactly do you mean by being in flow?" I asked. She said, "you know I'm manifesting, and everything I want is coming to me effortlessly, and I mean everything!" She rambled on about all the things that came to her in the past week, such as a new job, boyfriend, and so forth.

Jesus, what a talent! I thought to myself. I have obviously missed the boat, but I need this ability in my life!

"So, what exactly does it take to manifest?" I continued. "Well, all you really need to do is sit and visualize what you want. Then you repeatedly take the steps to get it," she explained. It is as simple as that.

I thought to myself, I must be a moron. All the times I wanted something and then took action to get it, I was only perhaps a hair away from achieving it. Why did I quit? I guess I must be impatient, and repetition is not my thing. Nevertheless, I was determined to catch the next boat. So off I went to practice, and practice I did.

A couple of weeks passed, and I needed to see Claudia. Once again, I struck out. My efforts yielded nothing. I needed something, or I would not see any results. Jealousy was driving me. I needed to learn about all the new things she attracted into her life since our last visit and how she did it. The suspense was killing me.

I knocked on her door, and she answered with tears in her eyes. "Oh my god, what's the matter?" I asked. Claudia blurted out that her dream job fell through, and Mr. Wonderful turned out to be Mr. Asshole and blah, blah, blah... She was no longer in the flow! Manifesting is a trickier business with more subtleties than either of us was aware of.

In any event, it would take years until I learned more about manifesting and flow. Claudia's experience turned out to be quite a common one. People often experience coincidental results from their efforts and attribute it to a unique ability, such as being in the flow. The following is one of my favorite anecdotes on being in the flow.

A man wakes up on the morning of his 55th birthday. He notices it is 5:55. He takes 55 minutes to eat and dress, then turns on the television and finds it on channel 5. The date is May 5th. He leaves his 5th-floor apartment, gets on the number 5 bus, and travels 5 miles to work. He takes the 5th elevator to the 5th floor of his office at 555

5th Street and notices there are five people on the elevator with him. He gets off and goes to the 5th door on the left of his office. Being a bright person, he notices all the coincidental events involving the number 5. He starts to wonder how he may take advantage of them. On his desk, he finds a racing form someone has left. He turns to the 5th page and finds that the 5th horse in the 5th race is named "Your Lucky 5s." He figures this must be the message. A surefire way to make money, so he calls the local bookie and places $5,000 on the race. He calls back at 5:00 p.m. and asks how his horse did. The bookie replies, "He came in 5th!"

Not in flow! All jokes aside, is being in the flow a real thing or just dreaming? The short answer is yes!

There are examples of people who experience flow states. People in different professions and contexts. For example, there are athletes that are training or playing, actors rehearsing or performing, business professionals executing their work, such as trading securities, and others.

What is most interesting is not all people that claim to be in flow are in a flow state. Claudia happened to be one of those people. Why? Because unknowingly, she had mistaken her mental absence and focus for a decrease in awareness. In other words, to be in Flow requires a certain amount of awareness to experience the energetic feeling and focus.

Claudia did not report such a feeling. She described the energetic feeling at the tail end of the activity. It was only when she emerged into consciousness. In other words, she experienced the feeling not during the process but after the process. She was being optimistic and hopeful that her thoughts would come true. I refer to it as auto-pilot because you are acting and performing without mental presence.

Another way to understand what I am describing is to think of Pavlov's dog experiments. Pavlov observed an interesting occurrence.

His dog subjects would commence salivating whenever an associate entered the room.

Pavlov and his associates would introduce a variety of edible and non-edible items and measure the saliva production of the items produced. He observed that salivation is a reflexive process. It automatically occurs in response to a certain stimulus and is not under conscious control.

However, he noted that the canines would often begin salivating in the absence of food and smell. He quickly realized this salivary response was a physiological process, not automatic. It is now commonly referred to as Classical conditioning or, as I call it, auto-pilot.

Classical conditioning is a type of unconscious or automatic learning. This learning process creates a conditioned response through associations between an unconditioned stimulus and a neutral stimulus.

In other words, classical conditioning involves placing a neutral stimulus before a naturally occurring reflex. In Pavlov's classic experiment with dogs, the neutral signal was the sound of a tone, and the naturally occurring reflex was salivating in response to food. By associating the neutral stimulus (sound) with the unconditioned stimulus (food), the sound of the tone alone could produce a salivation response.

An unconditioned stimulus is a stimulus or trigger that leads to an automatic response. If a cold breeze makes you shiver, for instance, the cold breeze is an unconditioned stimulus; it produces an involuntary response (the shivering).

A neutral stimulus is a stimulus that does not initially trigger a response. If you hear a fan but do not feel the breeze, it will not necessarily trigger a response. That would make it a neutral stimulus.

A conditioned stimulus is a stimulus that was once neutral (didn't trigger a response) but now leads to a response. If you previously did not pay attention to dogs but then got bit by one, and now you feel fear every time you see a dog, the dog has become a conditioned stimulus.

An unconditioned response is an automatic response or a response that occurs without thought when an unconditioned stimulus is present. If you smell your favorite food and your mouth starts watering, the watering is an unconditioned response.

A conditioned response is a learned response or a response that is created where no response existed before. Going back to the example of being bitten by a dog, the fear you experience after the bite is a conditioned response.

Classical conditioning involves forming an association between two stimuli, resulting in a learned response. There are three phases of this process.

The first part of the classical conditioning process requires a naturally occurring stimulus that will automatically elicit a response. Salivating in response to the smell of food is an example of a naturally occurring stimulus.

During this phase, the unconditioned stimulus (UCS) results in an unconditioned response (UCR). Presenting food (the UCS) naturally and automatically triggers a salivation response (the UCR).

At this point, there is also a neutral stimulus that produces no effect—yet. It is not until the neutral stimulus is paired with the UCS that it will come to evoke a response.

Let us take a closer look at the two critical components of this phase of classical conditioning:

- ☼ The unconditioned stimulus is one that unconditionally, naturally, and automatically triggers a response. For example, when you smell one of your favorite foods, you may immediately feel hungry. In this example, the smell of the food is the unconditioned stimulus.

- ☀ The unconditioned response is the unlearned response that occurs naturally in response to the unconditioned stimulus.[4] In our example, the feeling of hunger in response to the smell of food is the unconditioned response.

In the "before conditioning" phase, they pair an unconditioned stimulus with an unconditioned response. They then introduced a neutral stimulus.

During the second phase of the classical conditioning process, the previously neutral stimulus is repeatedly paired with the unconditioned stimulus. As a result of this pairing, an association between the previously neutral stimulus and the UCS is formed.

At this point, the once-neutral stimulus becomes known as the conditioned stimulus (CS). The subject has now been conditioned to respond to this stimulus. The conditioned stimulus is a previously neutral stimulus that, after becoming associated with the unconditioned stimulus, eventually comes to trigger a conditioned response.

In our earlier example, suppose that when you smelled your favorite food, you also heard a whistle. While the whistle is unrelated to the smell of the food, if the sound of the whistle were paired multiple times with the smell, the whistle sound would eventually trigger the conditioned response. In this case, the sound of the whistle is the conditioned stimulus.

The "during conditioning" phase involves repeatedly pairing a neutral stimulus with an unconditioned stimulus. Eventually, the neutral stimulus becomes the conditioned stimulus.

Once the association has been made between the UCS and the CS, presenting the conditioned stimulus alone will evoke a response—even without the unconditioned stimulus. The resulting response is known as the conditioned response (CR).

The conditioned response is the learned response to the previously neutral stimulus. In our example, the conditioned response would be feeling hungry when you hear the whistle.

In the "after-conditioning" phase, the conditioned stimulus alone triggers the conditioned response.

Behaviorists have described different phenomena associated with classical conditioning. These elements involve the initial establishment of the response, while others report the disappearance of a response. Here is a closer look at the five key principles of classical conditioning.

The acquisition is the initial stage of learning when a response is first established and gradually strengthened. During the acquisition phase of classical conditioning, a neutral stimulus is repeatedly paired with an unconditioned stimulus.

As you may recall, an unconditioned stimulus is something that naturally and automatically triggers a response without any learning. After we make an association, the subject will begin to emit a behavior in response to the previously neutral stimulus, which is now known as a conditioned stimulus. It is at this point that we can say that the response has been acquired.

Once the response has been established, you can gradually reinforce the response to make sure the behavior is well learned.[11]

Alternatively, there is a Flow known as flow states or Being in the Zone. The flow state is the optimal state of human consciousness.

The state was first named "flow" by psychologist Mihály Csíkszentmihályi in 1975. Research on flow states began to increase in the 1980s and 90s.

The term "flow" came from Csikszentmihalyi's survey subjects describing what their peak activities felt like. They all described similar "flowy" experiences where every action flowed seamlessly, effortlessly, from one thing to the next.

Csikszentmihalyi's research, along with other scientists, uncovered ten characteristics of the flow state.

Four of them are among "flow triggers," and they are found to precede flow.

The following flow triggers are not the only ones, but they have been found to help drive you into a flow state.

- Intense Concentration—not dividing your mind between tasks but being totally absorbed by one action in the present moment.
- Challenge/Skills Balance—the challenge of the task slightly exceeds your skill set. You are pushed out of your comfort zone. The magic ratio is about 4% harder than you are comfortable with. You want to stretch yourself—not snap.
- Clear Goals—not big life goals (like winning a gold medal or making a million dollars). Small, immediately achievable goals. Knowing where you are right now and where you want to go next.
- Immediate Feedback—closing the gap between cause and effect. In a moment, you can course correct mid-flight.

These characteristics help propel you into the flow. Check out this article for more flow triggers.

If you want to know if an experience qualifies as being in the flow state, this list of flow characteristics is a marvelous place to start.

- Action and Awareness Merge—You and what you are doing become one. Your actions feel automatic and require little or no additional resources.
- Selflessness—Your sense of self disappears. As self-consciousness goes away, the inner critic is silenced.

- Timelessness—You experience an altered perception of time. Past and future disappear as you enter "a deep now."
- Effortlessness—Your sense of struggle and frustration vanishes.
- Intrinsic Motivation—The experience is "autotelic." This means the activity has a purpose within itself. The activity or work becomes its own reward.
- Paradox of Control—You have a powerful sense of control over the situation. In flow, you are the expert in your own destiny.

These characteristics feel so good that the flow becomes addictive!

That is why you should pay attention to the flow cycle below. It is important to realize that we are not meant to be in flow all the time.

If you chase flow too much and become a "bliss junkie," you'll experience the dark side of the flow.

The two types of flow are individual and group.

To create more flow in your life, take this quiz to find out what's blocking your flow.

The shared, collective experience of a group performing at its peak is called "group flow."

If you're looking for some tips on creating more group flow, start with the following post on creativity in the workplace.

You also need to understand that flow has degrees of experience. When you are angry, you can feel anything from mildly ticked off to enraged.

You can also experience various levels of flow in your life.

Here are both ends of the flow spectrum:

- Micro-flow. Getting sucked into a great brainstorming conversation with someone.
- Macro-flow. All the above characteristics show up, and you're suddenly one with the universe.
- While there is no neurobiological definition of flow, Herb Benson's research at Harvard led to the understanding of the four stages of flow.

1. Struggle—this is the loading phase when you are overloading the brain with information. This would be a baseball pitcher learning a new pitch or a writer researching and diagramming a structure for a new book. It is important to remember that flow starts with this unpleasant state.
2. Release—take your mind off the problem. To get into the flow state, you are trading conscious processing for subconscious processing. Slow thinking with limited RAM for efficient endless RAM. To do that, you must stop thinking. Go for a long walk, garden, take a hot or cold shower, and stare at the clouds.
3. Flow state—stress hormones leave your system. They are replaced by feel-good neurochemicals. Flow demands laser-focused attention in the present. The brain trades energy normally used for other purposes and reallocates it for flow.
4. Recovery—at the end of the flow state is a critical recovery phase. After the amazing high of flow, you are going to crash. You need certain vitamins, minerals, and sunlight to get back. Steven Kotler says, "If you really want to hack flow, you're going to need to learn how to struggle better and how to recover better."

You need to develop grit to take all the stages of the flow cycle seriously.

If you get stressed out by the struggle or recovery phase, you are going to produce too much cortisol. This will block the deep learning that is meant to happen during flow. You may still get a short-term benefit, but the long-term benefits of a high-flow lifestyle will be lost.

Also, you might think that vegging out in front of the television counts as recovery. It does not. Screen time produces waves in the brain that block flow.[12]

Flow states are invaluable and can help you dramatically. However, it is imperative that you approach it scientifically and monitor what you are doing. You want to be sure you are truly experiencing flow and not something else, like my friend Claudia.

Chapter 7

Everyone Has The Same Single Greatest Challenge.

"Challenges are what make life interesting, and overcoming them is what makes life meaningful."

—Joshua J. Marine

In my previous book, I talked about one of the toughest challenges I faced in my career. I was in trouble financially and needed help fast. It was before when the internet and access to information were scarce. I had nowhere to turn except the place I despised the most, the bookstore.

I absolutely became ill at the thought of reading, but I was out of options. I desperately needed information and needed it yesterday. So, I caved in and trekked on over to the nearest Barnes & Noble. I began walking the isles, hoping and trusting I would find a book that could answer my prayers.

There I found books that intimidated me and put my greatest weakness to the test, reading. As much as I doubted my ability to read such lengthy books, I also feared failure. They were equally haunting, yet I knew with certainty either one or the other was going to prevail.

In my case, I did, in fact, find what I needed. It was easier to find the books than I had anticipated. However, reading the books was not so easy, but still easier than I envisioned. I not only found what I needed but also learned a great deal about my fear of reading and other things along the way.

What is your single biggest challenge? Your career? A relationship? Money? Attention? Credibility? Love? Lacking a skill? Are you sure? Guess again! Did you change your answer? Now guess again. Are you still wrong? Want to try again?

As I continue my travels from country to country, I enjoy asking people this question. So, tell me… what is your single biggest challenge?

Because, without variance, one out of every fifty people will respond immediately with the correct answer. It does not matter whether I am in London, Miami, Hong Kong, Moscow, Tulum, Rio de Janeiro, or Medellin, men or women, young or old, results are the same.

So, what is it? Well, I am certain if you have not figured it out, you will before you finish the chapter. The reason I am so certain is that if you have read this far, you have a thirst for knowledge. A thirst for the truth. Most importantly, you enjoy a challenge, thinking, expanding your mind, and personal growth. You are the type of person that can and will get it on your own accord.

You will find articles all over the internet that suggest all sorts of culprits from an early age, failing to act timely, relationships, what others think, toxic people, fear, negativity, the past, the future, the environment, and so forth. However, it all boils down to one thing. And one thing only!

KISS! Yes, one of my favorite sayings because, timelessly, it proves true. <u>K</u>eep <u>I</u>t <u>S</u>imple <u>S</u>tupid! We like to think we are special, we are unique, and sometimes that is true. However, in this matter, we are all the same. So, do not overthink it, KISS, accept it.

Because once you do, you will have the most important and impressive piece of knowledge you will need to succeed. Yes, you heard me right! Answer the question correctly, and you will have the most important and powerful piece of knowledge you will need to succeed! Feel the pressure?

How do I know I am right in my assertion of such a bold claim? It's for two reasons. First, people agree the statement is correct once they reflect on it. And second, I know you will too!

I am curious when you begin to think of the answer to my question. Are you thinking about yourself? I did ask you what is your single biggest challenge? So, why am I now asking you this question instead of what is the single greatest challenge everyone has? It is because I demand you get the answer, and we need to start somewhere simple. And that just so happens to be with you.

I am now going to share a true story with you. A story that I will briefly mention at the end of the chapter to show you that even under the most extreme situations, my statement remains valid.

I'M FOREWARNING YOU.

THE FOLLOWING STORY MAY TERRIFY YOU!!!

YOU MAY FIND IT DISTURBING, AND EVEN HAUNTING!!!

IT IS SOMETHING THAT NO ONE WOULD EVER WISH TO EXPERIENCE. SO, IF YOU ARE AN OBSESSIVE-COMPULSIVE PERSON OR EASILY SCARED, YOU MAY WANT TO JUMP PAST THE BOLD HEADING ENTITLED "END OF STORY." ALSO, THE NAME OF THE PERSONS, LOCATIONS, AND LANDMARK NAMES ARE CHANGED TO PROTECT THE IDENTITY OF THE INDIVIDUAL INVOLVED.

For context, I will briefly set the stage. I was in a foreign country where people spoke little to no English. I was there on a business trip, and a friend who is an international public figure came to visit. He stayed at a hotel that happened to be a handful of miles from where I was staying.

We communicated via WhatsApp and agreed to meet for dinner and listen to live music afterward. As it turned out, unfortunately, we were unable to meet for dinner but settled to meet at a music venue. We were both anxiously looking forward to listening to live local music.

We arrived at the venue ten to fifteen minutes apart and got a table close to the stage. We each had a beer and enjoyed the crowd as well as the music for one hour. We then decided to leave in hopes of something a little more exciting.

He ordered an Uber, and we headed into town by his hotel. We decided to walk around and see more of the town. It was a quiet night, so at 11:00 pm, we agreed to call it a night. He waited with me on the street corner until my Uber arrived. I got in the car, and I watched him head off toward his hotel. It was a mere three blocks away.

At 11:00 am the following morning, my cellphone rang.

"Hi, is this Keith?"

I recognized my friend's voice, and I laughed, "what's up?"

He asked, "where are you?"

"I'm at my place, and what about you?"

He said, "are you nearby?"

I laughed and said, "well, it all depends on where you are."

He replied, "I am not sure. Someone drugged me. Can you come over now?"

I said, "sure, but can you look around to see if there is something that indicates you are at your hotel or somewhere else?"

He replied, "I'm at the Excelsior."

"Do not move. I will be there in 10 minutes". My heart was racing as I ordered an Uber, put on my shoes, slipped my wallet into my pocket, and ran for the ride.

Within moments of entering the Uber, my phone rang. It was my friend. "Hi, is this Keith?" he said.

"Yes, I am on my way. I will be there in a couple minutes."

"Ok, I'm in my room," he replied.

Within minutes, I arrived at the hotel. I stormed the lobby to reach the front desk. I told the gentlemen behind the counter that I had an emergency and that I needed him to escort me to my friend's room immediately, which he did.

When we went to his room, the door was wide open, and he was standing in his underwear, dazed and confused.

He looked at me and said, "who are you?"

I looked at the gentleman that was with me, but he spoke no English and had no idea what was going on. I was as confused as the two of them.

I turned to my friend and said, "Everett, It's me, Keith."

"Do I know you?" he stammered.

I had never witnessed anything like this. I had no experience and no one to help. All I could think of was to remain calm for everyone's sake.

"Everett, let us sit down for a moment. Do you mind if I look around to see if anyone has been here in your room?"

"No, go ahead."

I quickly looked around for anything to indicate that someone had been in his room, but there was nothing of the sort. I could see his laptop in plain sight sitting on the desk. I checked the safe near his computer, and it was sealed shut.

He asked me, "so, how do I know you?"

It was impossible for me to think clearly! I had so many questions myself, but I knew he would not be able to answer any of them. I sat him down and explained to him who I was and that he was visiting for three days.

He then asked me the following questions:

1. My name is Everett Evanston, right?
2. Where am I?
3. You're Keith and a friend of mine, correct?
4. Where do I live?
5. Why are you here?
6. Where are my wallet and cell phone?

I answered each question as follows:

1. Yes, your name is Everett.
2. You are in Oslo visiting for three days.
3. Yes, I am Keith, and we are longtime friends from Los Angeles.
4. You currently live in London.
5. I am here because you called me to come over so we could hang out while you are in town.
6. Your wallet is locked in the safe. But do not worry. It is not going anywhere because you cannot remember the combination. And your cell phone is in your hand.

With each question I answered, Everett replied, "thank you, Keith, for being such a good friend. I really appreciate it!"

All I could think was, "what the hell should I do next?" No sooner than the thought crossed my mind, he asked the same six questions all over again in the same order. I could see he was determined to get answers.

I answered the questions and then interjected, "can you remember the last person you saw?" He could not. He could not remember who he saw last, his family members, or even the answer to the last question he asked. It was as if his memory was completely erased. The whole thing was straight out of a movie, but nothing I had ever seen in real life.

I decided to try to take a quick assessment of the entire situation. I asked him to examine himself in the bathroom to see if he had any injuries or even any indication that he had sex.

While he went to the bathroom, it dawned on me that it would be best to see if he was experiencing any physical impairment that could be life-threatening. I happen to be certified as a Search and Rescue Scuba Diver, which required a significant amount of emergency first aid training.

I felt confident if I could get a better read on his vital signs, I could make a reasonable determination whether to take him to the hospital. It was not my first choice. I knew taking him to a hospital in a foreign country where he would not understand what was going on could add to his trauma. It was the first tricky decision I made.

Within a matter of minutes, he emerged from the bathroom and asked me what I was doing there. I told him he asked me to stop by to hang out. I did not want to alarm him. I looked him in the eyes and, in a subtle way, had him demonstrate to me that he was okay. He then when back to the six questions.

I said, "how about I answer your questions on the way to the restaurant downstairs so I can get something to eat?" He said sure, and we headed for the door. "Not so fast, Everett! You should put on clothes first."

"Yeah, okay, where are they," as he moped around the room.

I managed to get him down to the restaurant as he continued with the six questions in the same order. It became apparent he was not giving up. We made it to a table, and I said, "Everett, I need to talk with you for a minute."

"I am not sure what is going on with you. I suppose it is possible someone drugged you. However, you look fine, and it does not make sense. For instance, why would someone drug you? Second, if it was their intent to take advantage of you, that does not appear to be the case. Nothing is missing, and no one assaulted you."

"I believe with time, we will get a better understanding of what transpired. Rather than assume you have a physiological ailment affecting your brain, let us go with the assumption that it is a drug and less severe. Drugs take time to wear off, so I recommend you consume as an abundance of fluids as possible to dilute the effects. Can you do that for me?"

He replied, "Well, I'm not really thirsty," and then launched back into the six questions. There was no stopping or diverting him. He was caught in a loop and needed his answers. The crazy part is that nothing I gave him was recorded in his memory. He was getting frustrated not knowing what was going on, and I answered his six questions repeatedly.

I did not want to add any additional stress for fear things could get worse. So, I did my best to remain calm and continued to answer the questions. An hour passed, and nothing changed. Despite my clever attempts at cajoling him, he had not touched the water or juice in front of him.

I had an idea. "Hey, Everett, I need to get Gatorade because I am feeling dehydrated. There is a store three blocks away. How about we take a short walk?"

"Ok, sure!" He replied. "My name is Everett Evanston, right?"

"Yes, it is!"

"Where am I?"

"Again? With the questions? This is crazy," I thought!

We headed out, and I answered his six questions repetitiously along the way. Eventually, we arrived at the store. I convinced him to have a Gatorade with me as I stocked up with as much as I could carry. It was now 12:30 pm, and I was totally spent.

"Everett, I have another idea! Let us go back to your place and get your things, and you can come stay at my place while we figure everything out. Sound good?"

"Sure!" He replied. "My name is Everett Evanston, right?"

The six questions continued as we returned to his hotel, packed up his things, and headed to my place. We dropped off his belongings at my place, and I convinced him to go food shopping, so we would have food and drinks so we would not need to move around too much. All the while, he continued with the six questions.

It was now 2:20 pm, and still not an ounce of improvement. Everett had no idea what was going on. Nevertheless, a part of me was terrified that he may have a severe brain disorder. The consequences of which would be devastating and horrifying. It was too much to consider.

I dashed the thought and focused on the lesser of two evils, being drugged. With that in mind, I had faith the effects would eventually fade and his memory would return. However, admittedly, it was mere speculation and dreaming. We sat in my living room, and I continued to answer the six questions repeatedly. It was fatiguing! At one point, I began laughing because I could not imagine the whole thing was real. I sat shaking my head, thinking, why me? Why him? Why us? How much more? The time passed as if minutes were days.

It was now 11:00 pm, and — God is my witness — I had answered his six questions more than 300 times at my last count. More than 1800 questions, Everett replied to every single one of those questions with, "thank you, Keith, for being such a good friend. I really appreciate it!"

I could not keep the count anymore or my eyes open any longer. I needed sleep, but I could not leave him for fear something awful might happen. What if he freaks out and jumps off the balcony? It's twenty-five stories, and I could not live with that. What if he slips out the door and into the night and gets lost? I would not have the stamina for the search and rescue.

I need to tough this one out! I served to him, "Everett, I need to lay down in my bed. Do not go anywhere! I am going to leave the door to my room open. If you need anything, just get me."

"Sure!" He replied. "My name is Everett Evanston, right?" With the other questions in tow.

I headed for a pit stop in the bathroom. As I exited the bathroom, he was in the doorway, back at it with the questions. I answered them and then escorted him to the guest bedroom and asked him to lie down and rest, and he did.

I went back to my bedroom, and before my head hit the pillow, he was in the doorway asking questions. I answered him and then asked him to please go lie down. To his credit, he agreed, turned around, and went to his room. However, he closed my bedroom door.

What the fuck? You must be kidding me. I do my best not to use profanity, but I frankly lost my mental composure. The lack of sleep took its toll on me. I physically could not get up.

What should I do? It was now more than 12 hours with absolutely zero improvements. And not a single question of mine answered, "Could he still be in danger? Does he pose a threat to himself?" I thought. "I cannot get up! I cannot get up!" I was done!

With my mind swirling, there was a knock on the door. Everett cracked open the door and said, "hey Keith can I talk with you?" I sprung out of bed. My eyes almost left my face. It was the first time he did something other than ask the six questions.

"Come in, come in, and leave the door open!" Everett went on to say, "so I am Everett Evanston, I am in Oslo, and you are my friend Keith. I live in London, but I am visiting with you in Oslo, and we think I may have been drugged."

Unbelievable! It is now 1:30 am, and he finally did something different! More than fourteen hours later! I cannot believe it!

Everett spent the day struggling to remember whatever he could. It took more than fourteen hours for him to have a shift. Throughout the day, I encouraged him not to think. I repeatedly explained to him that if you are under the influence of a drug, chances are nothing will change until the drug wears off. So, try not to stress yourself by trying to remember anything.

However, habits are hard to break! Human conditioning can be so strong that we are not even aware of what we are doing. Everett lost his ability to remember anything. And, despite how desperately he tried to remember, he simply could not. His conditioning took over and dominated his mental absence.

Over the next hour, Everett repeatedly came back to my room for the six questions. On his 12th entry, he exclaimed, "I feel like I have done this before. Have I come into your room before to ask you a question?"

"Yes, you have! Twelve times to be exact."

"Has it been that many times?" he asked.

"Yup! How about you try to sleep?"

He agreed, and I rose out of bed. I showed him to his room and waited for him to get in bed. I turned off the lights and, upon my exit, softly heard the words, "thank you, Keith, for being such a good friend. I really appreciate it!"

"You got it!"

I returned to my room, slid into bed, extinguished the lights, and sat in darkness until 3:30 am. I then heard a knock on the door. I flung open my eyes. It was Everett in the doorway, and it was as light as day. In fact, it was! It was now 9:30 am, and Everett looked and spoke as if he had an epic hangover.

"Keith, what am I doing here? Where exactly are we? Can you tell me what is going on? I feel hungover and confused."

Everett's awareness was returning! "How about we get dressed and talk over breakfast?"

"Sure" replied Everett.

Everett insisted we spend the entire day testing and exercising his memory. I did not agree with his choice, but under the circumstances felt it best to support Everett's decisions. It was slow, tedious, and exhausting as we attempted to piece together the previous 48 hours in hopes of finding critical answers.

It would take a third day for us to gain clarity on all of Everett's movements. We were able to do so by tapping into the APPs on his cellphone. Between his phone and mine, we pieced together every movement he made except for two hours. Two hours were right before I received his initial call.

Our theory that someone drugged him at the music venue failed. And so did the theory that someone dosed him upon his return to the hotel that same night. However, we were able to deduce that someone had dosed him the morning he called me. He then was able to make it back to his hotel room and pass out for two hours.

We also discovered with great certainty who committed the crime but could not confirm the substance used. I am happy to report that after Everett extended his stay, he was well enough to travel and return home. He soon thereafter made a full recovery, except for his memory of that frightening 24-hour period, which he still lacks today.

"END OF STORY"

If you were brave enough to read the story of Everett, I will now ask you the following: What is Everyone's Single Greatest Challenge?

In case you did not read the story or you are not certain your answer is correct, we will briefly cover other examples. It is vital that you get the correct answer to the question if you want to succeed as quickly as possible. In fact, people do fail altogether because they never get the answer to this question.

We may not always realize it, but life's limitations can sometimes inspire us to strive for heights we may not have reached otherwise. The most successful people in the world have overcome tremendous obstacles to reach their goals.

For instance, Steven Hawking was diagnosed with ALS at an early age. Hawking ranked third from the bottom of his class in high school and only gave the minimum amount of time to his studies in college before he got ill.

He felt he still had time left and took a new interest in his studies and research. "I was bored with life before my illness," he said. "There had not seemed to be anything worth doing." His illness sparked him to achieve even more than he may have reached without his illness. Hawking has said, "although there was a cloud hanging over my future, I found, to my surprise, that I was enjoying life in the present more than before."

Once diagnosed with ALS, Hawking started studying black holes and the origins of the universe. As his health declined, he began using a wheelchair, and his life and research flourished.

His research garnered public attention in 1974, showing that black holes are not information gobblers as previously thought. Instead, they emit particle streams. His "Hawking Radiation" discovery provided essential information about how gravity relates to forms of energy.

His discovery and publications made him a worldwide sensation, and he was named a fellow of the Royal Society. He also earned the Albert Einstein Award and the Pius XI Gold Medal for Science from Pope Paul VI. His subsequent theories continue to further the world's understanding of the universe.

"I am quite often asked: 'How do you feel about having ALS?' The answer is not a lot," Hawking said. "I try to lead as normal a life as possible and not think about my condition or regret the things it prevents me from doing, which are not that many."

Hawking beat the odds of living only an additional ten years. "I have been lucky that my condition has progressed more slowly than is often the case," Hawking said. "But it shows that one need not lose hope."

Hawking is an inspiration to many, notably those facing a challenging chronic or serious illness. His positive thinking and focus on what can be done, managing time, and ignoring hurdles can be taught in all areas of life.

Next up is Oprah Winfrey. Oprah's mother was a single teenage mom on welfare. Oprah was passed around between her mother, grandmother, and father while living in poverty.

She was abused and beaten regularly and recanted stories of being whipped until she bled. She regularly experienced loneliness. At nine years old, she was raped by her 19-year-old cousin and continued to suffer sexual abuse from other relatives until she was 13 years when she decided to run away from home. At 14, she became pregnant, and soon after the baby's birth, it died.

However, her grandmother taught her to read at an early age, and her father made education a priority. "My father turned my life around by insisting that I be more than I was. His love of learning showed me the way."

She attended Nashville East High School and took public speaking and drama. She was elected school president and received a full scholarship to Tennessee State University. She had a few broadcasting gigs and was named the talk show host for *People Are Talking*. From there, she landed a job as the host of *A.M. Chicago*. It became the highest-rated talk show in Chicago and was eventually renamed *The Oprah Winfrey Show*.

"I am so grateful for my years literally living in poverty," she said in an interview, "because it makes the experience of creating success and building success that much more rewarding." Oprah went on to create the monthly magazine, O, The Oprah Magazine. She also produced films, syndicated television programs, and a Broadway musical. She got nominated for Best Supporting Actress for her role in *The Color Purple*.

In 2011 she launched her cable network, OWN. She has been called the "world's most powerful woman" and has appeared on *Time*'s "100 most influential" list ten times since 2004. From 2004 until 2010, she gave away close to $400 million to educational causes.

Studies show that positivity can produce beneficial results such as less stress, better-coping skills, and increased health. Oprah continues to support positive thinking and has devoted many of her programs to this topic.

"The greatest discovery of all time," she said, "is that a person can change his future by merely changing his attitude." A person's situation has much to do with their well-being, state of mind, and attitude.

Oprah's quest for self-realization and courage to share her life experience is why millions love and respect her! It explains how she achieved so much in an abbreviated period. It is also responsible for her wild success.

When she realized "The greatest discovery of all time," she also discovered that "Everyone Has the Same Single Greatest Challenge!"

If you have not realized it by now, it is OURSELVES!

Yes, "Everyone Has the Same Single Greatest Challenge!" It is OURSELVES!

When Steven Hawkins accepted his diagnosis and decided not to be consumed by it and instead focus on what was possible is when his career exploded.

Similarly, Oprah chose not to let the abuse and trauma she suffered define her. Instead, she chose to focus on her education and how to rise to greater heights.

We are the ones that place limitations and obstacles on ourselves. In the case of my dear friend Everett, no matter how hard he tried to recall events, it was hopeless. The harder he tried, the more frustrated and tired he became.

Only with brief periods of rest was Everett able to recall things. Sure, you could blame it on the drug, but regardless, he needed to get out of his way to get back his memory. He was partially responsible for the speed of his progress.

Have you ever decided to go on a diet and lose 10-20 pounds? Everything starts great, and then you begin to waiver, cheat, or even give up. How about quitting smoking? You get the patch or other aid. Everything is going hunky dory until something stressful happens, you get rattled, and you say give me a cigarette. Next thing you know, you are done! How about cutting or quitting alcohol? What about a plan to build a business? How about an exercise plan?

We all have the tendency to sabotage ourselves! We are not all perfect with sufficient motivation or willpower to withstand every test we are given. If we know it to be the case, it is an opportunity for us to be more mindful of our negative actions, master them, and achieve our goals. You can achieve remarkable things and even what seems unobtainable if you know your greatest challenge is yourself and moving out of your way!

Chapter 8

You Have Access to More Knowledge Than You Need.

"We're surrounded by data, but starved for insights."

—Jay Baer-

As I mentioned in Chapter 4, the amount of estimated data in the world in 2020 was 44 zettabytes. And by 2025, the amount of data generated each day is expected to reach 463 exabytes globally.

Those 44 zettabytes are equivalent to 44,000,000,000 terabytes, but remember, your brain can only retain somewhere between 10-100 terabytes. Importantly, the information we are discussing is "recorded data." It only represents a small amount of all the information in recorded history. And there is an incalculable amount of information we have yet to record and discover.

In other words, a ridiculous amount of recorded data and incalculable information & experiences yet to be captured surrounds us. Each one of us only gets to encounter an infinitesimal portion of each during our lifetime. Therefore, we can agree we have access to more knowledge than needed to solve a problem or challenge, and trying to memorize as much as we can is pointless.

However, it is wonderful news because now there is one less thing to think about. One less barrier to overcome, less stress! Somewhere out there, the solution exists. The big question is how do we capture the valuable information relevant to our situation?

How did Gandhi, Galileo, Muhammad, Sun Tzu, or any other famous person produce something brilliant? Have you ever given it thought? Seriously, give the question thought for a moment. We know it is not luck!

So, how did they get the thought? How do you get the thought you need? What is a thought? Bet you never even gave it any thought!

It is a fair question because thoughts are abstract and complex; they are not visible. So, here is the answer that will help you get what you need.

Thoughts are electrochemical reactions. The human brain is composed of about 100 billion nerve cells (neurons) interconnected by trillions of connections called synapses. On average, each connection transmits about one signal per second. Some specialized connections send up to 1,000 signals per second. "Somehow… that's producing thought," says Charles Jennings, director of neurotechnology at the MIT McGovern Institute for Brain Research.

Given the physical complexity of what's happening inside your head, it's not easy to trace a thought from beginning to end. "That's a little like asking where the forest begins. Is it with the first leaf or the tip of the first root?" says Jennings. Simpler, then to start by considering perceptions — "thoughts" that are directly triggered by external stimuli—a feather brushes your skin, you see these words on the computer screen, you hear a phone ring. Each of these events triggers a series of signals in the brain.

Consider this?!

When you read these words, for example, the photons associated with the patterns of the letters hit your retina, and their energy triggers an electrical signal in the light-detecting cells. That electrical signal propagates like a wave along the long threads called axons that are part of the connections between neurons. When the signal reaches the end of an axon, it causes the release of chemical neurotransmitters into the synapse, a chemical junction between the axon tip and target neurons. A target neuron responds with its electrical signal, which, in turn, spreads to other neurons. Within a few hundred milliseconds, the signal has spread to billions of neurons in several dozen interconnected areas of your brain, and you have perceived these words. (All that, and you probably didn't even break a sweat.)

The fact that you are then able to convert the perception of these shapes into symbols, language, and meaning is a whole other story—and a good indication of the complexity of neuroscience. Trying to imagine how trillions of connections and billions of simultaneous transmissions coalesce inside your brain to form a thought is a little like trying to look at the leaves, roots, snakes, birds, ticks, deer—and everything else in a forest—at the same moment.[13]

According to the director of neurotechnology at MIT, the process is complex. The explanation proffered includes the idea information already exists in fragments. It then coalesces into a full-blown thought when a stimulus is introduced. It is then absorbed and transmitted through neurons. The director provides a wonderful explanation, and it is certainly one possibility.

We are going to run with the director's explanation for the moment and drill down to the information. What is information? It is an abstract concept. It is the interpretation of what may be sensed. In other words, knowledge is obtained from investigation, study, or instruction. You get the point! It is an interpretation that comes from the data we receive. Data that already exists!

So, how do we get it? The same way we get a cocktail, wisdom, a kiss, influenza, money, or anything else. Care to take a guess? The answer is remarkably simple!

It is transferred to us.

And how exactly is it transferred to us?

Resonance!

An easy example to understand is resonance energy transfer in photosynthesis. Do you remember photosynthesis from grade school? The process by which plants use sunlight, water, and carbon dioxide to create oxygen and energy in the form of sugar.

What is resonance energy transfer in photosynthesis? In this fashion, energy is transferred from one chlorophyll to another. This type of energy transfer is called resonance energy transfer or exciton transfer.

What is resonance energy transfer in biology? Resonance energy transfer (RET, also known as fluorescence resonance energy transfer, FRET, or electronic energy transfer, EET) is an optical process in which the excess energy of an excited molecule—usually called the donor—is transferred to an acceptor molecule.[14]

Familiar with Tesla? No, not the car. I am referring to Nikola Tesla, the inventor, electrical & mechanical engineer, and futurist. Tesla is famous for demonstrating that energy may be transmitted wirelessly.

In today's terms, think Bluetooth. Bluetooth uses radio waves to exchange data between fixed and mobile devices over short distances. For instance, wireless headphones allow you to listen to music on your laptop or phone without the limitation of wires.

Tesla also studied electromagnetic resonance. Resonance occurs when a system can store and transfer energy between two or more different storage modes (such as kinetic energy and potential energy in the case of a simple pendulum).[15]

Consider this?!

Are you familiar with Elon Musk's latest project, Neuralink? Neuralink is a device, or a Brain-Machine Interface (BMI), to be specific. The BMI is surgically implanted into the human brain, which can be a means of communication between humans and machines. <u>Humans can even control these machines only by *thinking* up a single command</u>. Neuralink also helps with the study and research of cures for various medical problems by allowing the transfer of data emitted from the body back to a digital receiver.

What Transfers the Brain Data?

Ever since the establishment of the company in 2016, they have been continuously developing this technology. The Neuralink chipset, also known as the N1 chipset, measures 8mm in diameter, with several wires housing electrodes and necessary insulation for these wires.

These wires are surgically implanted into the brain via a robot. The company claims the wires are as thick as the neurons in the brain and are 100 micrometers in diameter. That's thinner than a strand of hair! The interesting part is that more than one of these devices can be placed in the skull to target different sections of the brain.

Neuralink can send and receive electrical signals through the brain to control machines. Because of this, the company says we can be able to control basic devices like smartphones and computers and even type using our thoughts.

Now, for us to understand how Neuralink works, we should know our brain sends information to different parts of the body, 24/7, via neurons. The neurons in your brain are connected to form an extensive network and communicate with chemical signals known as neurotransmitters. This reaction creates an electric field and is marked by placing electrodes within a close distance. These electrodes understand the electric signals passing through the brain and translate them into an algorithm the machine can read. Through this process,

Neuralink can read what we're thinking and find a way for us to interact with the machines without even talking.

For now, Neuralink is making use of Bluetooth.

The company says it will only use the initial phase of the project in the healthcare industry. The machine will aid paraplegics with simple tasks like operating a phone or computer. It might also be used later to treat epilepsy. During an interview, Musk even said the machine could help people regain their eyesight even after losing their optic nerve. He said that this technology, theoretically, will be able to fix anything wrong with the brain. Musk also said that Neuralink could restore the speech, movement, and memory of a paralyzed person. With a complete symbiosis of the tech and the human brain, Musk states that it can be possible for humans to interact with each other without actually having to speak. Can you imagine that? A fantasy phenomenon coming to real life! We can also get additional hardware to stream music in our brains.[16]

In the passage above, it states, "These electrodes understand the electric signals passing through the brain and translate them into an algorithm the machine can read." What does this sound like to you? Does it sound like tuning your brain like a radio to a frequency to send a signal to communicate with another device to get information or music?

Musk is telling us that with the aid of Neuralink, we can transmit information from our brain to a computer and back wirelessly. Not only is he telling us we can do it, but he has proven it. He is also about to monetize his idea and make big money.

News Flash! Neuralink is a wonderful device that undoubtedly solves problems that are complex and is a solution for damaged pathways. However, when we are talking about capturing data on a microscopic scale, we do not need Neuralink implanted in our brain unless it is to replace a damaged pathway.

Think about it for a minute. In the case of data, it is analogous to sending Uber Eats to the local convenience store to get a pizza that sits in the cold section they purchased from Domino's Pizza. Is it necessary to get Uber and the convenience store involved when you could buy the pizza directly from Domino's, hot and ready to eat?

In other words, there is no reason for the two intermediaries. The two intermediaries refer to the Neuralink and the remote computer. Yes, I am suggesting we have the ability to capture data from anywhere without the need for a Nueralink, computer, or anything else.

Since you now have a better understanding of resonance energy transfer, I will share something called string theory, innovative physics.

In physics, string theory is a theoretical framework in which the point-like particles of particle physics are replaced by one-dimensional objects called strings. String theory describes how these strings propagate through space and interact with each other. On distance scales larger than the string scale, a string looks just like an ordinary particle, with its mass, charge, and other properties determined by the vibrational state of the string. In string theory, one of the many vibrational states of the string corresponds to the graviton, a quantum mechanical particle that carries the gravitational force. Thus, string theory is a theory of quantum gravity.

String theory is a broad and varied subject that attempts to address a number of deep questions of fundamental physics. String theory has contributed a number of advances to mathematical physics, which have been applied to a variety of problems in black hole physics, early universe cosmology, nuclear physics, and condensed matter physics, and it has stimulated a number of major developments in pure mathematics. Because string theory potentially provides a unified description of gravity and particle physics, it is a candidate for a theory of everything, a self-contained mathematical model that describes all fundamental forces and forms of matter. Despite much work on these problems, it is not known to what extent string theory describes the real world or how much freedom the theory allows in the choice of its details.

String theory was first studied in the late 1960s as a theory of the strong nuclear force before being abandoned in favor of quantum chromodynamics. Subsequently, it was realized that the properties that made string theory unsuitable as a theory of nuclear physics made it a promising candidate for a quantum theory of gravity. The earliest version of string theory, bosonic string theory, incorporated only the class of particles known as bosons. It later developed into superstring theory, which posits a connection called supersymmetry between bosons and the class of particles called fermions. Five consistent versions of superstring theory were developed before it was conjectured in the mid-1990s that they were all different limiting cases of a single theory in 11 dimensions known as M-theory. In late 1997, theorists discovered an important relationship called the anti-de Sitter/conformal field theory correspondence (AdS/CFT correspondence), which relates string theory to another type of physical theory called quantum field theory.

One of the challenges of string theory is that the full theory does not have a satisfactory definition in all circumstances. Another issue is that the theory is thought to describe an enormous landscape of possible universes, which has complicated efforts to develop theories of particle physics based on string theory. These issues have led some in the community to criticize these approaches to physics and to question the value of continued research on string theory unification.[17]

If you are confused, no worries. In short, on the smallest scale, everything is made of vibrating strings, including data. Resonance occurs with all types of vibration. In other words, the Strings or data vibrate and produce a frequency like a radio wave. Therefore, data is detectable. It is how your radio captures a song, your phone a call, and your computer a movie from Netflix. It is also how Neuralink works. The key to it all is being able to detect the data.

If you want the data, you should also be able to get it like your laptop gets information from the internet. Again, I ask the question, "how did we come up with the idea for the computer?" It is a replica of a human brain!

Your brain has the same capability as a laptop and more. The difference is your laptop comes with an Operations Manual, and your brain does not. However, some people know how it works. It explains how computers came into existence.

Resonance explains how people like Einstein make brilliant discoveries and how ordinary everyday people get an idea. They are simply capturing data they are detecting and processing it.

Arguably, another way to capture data is using the Law of Attraction. It is the New Thought spiritual belief that positive or negative thoughts bring positive or negative experiences into a person's life. The belief is based on the idea that people and their thoughts are made from "pure energy" and that energy can attract like energy, thereby allowing people to improve their health, wealth, or personal relationships. There is no empirical scientific evidence supporting the Law of Attraction, and it is widely considered to be pseudoscience.

Advocates generally combine cognitive reframing techniques with affirmations and creative visualization to replace limiting or self-destructive ("negative") thoughts with more empowered, adaptive ("positive") thoughts. A key component of the philosophy is the idea that in order to effectively change one's negative thinking patterns, one must also "feel" (through creative visualization) that the desired changes have already occurred. This combination of positive thought and positive emotion is believed to allow one to attract positive experiences and opportunities by achieving resonance with the proposed energetic law.

Supporters of the Law of Attraction refer to scientific theories and use them as arguments in favor of it. However, it has no demonstrable scientific basis. A number of researchers have criticized the misuse of scientific concepts by its proponents.[18]

Okay, you got me! The Law of Attraction is arguably a pseudoscience. I do not blame you if you do not believe in the Law of Attraction. I completely understand. I studied biochemistry, physics, and other sciences in college, not business. I believe in science and the scientific method, and I want proof that something exists.

We know, from experience, much of what we learn is false. Also, it takes time for science to validate theories. But a lack of validation doesn't mean it doesn't exist or is invalid or anything else. It only means it is yet to be scientifically proven.

If you believe in Physics, Consciousness, The Laws of Thermodynamics, Quantum Mechanics, and Entanglement, then you believe in energy, and everything is made of it. It took decades to validate these scientific disciplines and theories. String theory is next on the horizon, and possibly the Law of Attraction.

Regardless of whether you believe in the Law of Attraction. Data is energy, and it is out there. But where out there? If you believe in innovative science, it is in the Block Universe or the Quantum Field. We touched on the Block Universe early.

The Quantum Field looks like a train wreck jumble of symbols, mathematical formulae, and something one might find written on the walls of a UFO. We humans still attempt to make sense of it. Quantum Field Theory begins with particles and how they relate to each other. The basic foundation of it has to do with the knowledge that things around us, even the parts of our body, can be analyzed by looking at the atoms that make them up and how those atoms behave with other atoms to make up parts of a whole, something with which we are familiar. We analyze things in this way to understand events and happenings, phenomena and entities that occur constantly. Quantum Physicists endeavor to explain how basic building blocks of matter behave and to comprehend the laws that fully govern that behavior. In essence, this is where the Quantum Field Theory begins.

Given that it is this complex, one might think experiments would be flawed and unyielding when attempting to apply Quantum Field Theory to phenomena. You would be wrong. Quantum Field Theory has predicted many discoveries, the Higgs Boson particle, for example, and antimatter. It has also made unifying the different quantum theoretical laws that apply to different events, a reality, in a way. We can begin to examine things using Quantum Field Theory because it tells us that matter is not really a set of particles, per se, but more akin to a series of blanketed fields that overlap and bump together, forming matter and all we see around us. The specifics have not been isolated, nor have we even begun to scratch the surface of fully understanding Quantum Field Theory. When Paul Dirac, the first scientist to propose its existence in the 1920s, first realized the theoretical underpinnings of QFT, one would imagine that he knew that it would be far-reaching and paradigm-shifting. We see now that it has been. Using Dirac's ideas, we have probed further into the meaning of existence and why matter behaves as it does. In a sense, this makes the continued study of Quantum Field Theory all the more valuable. It may someday provide answers to our most fundamental questions about life, the universe, and even the beginning of all things.[19]

In conclusion, science offers us possibilities that explain where data lies, and wherever it may be, it is still in the form of energy. According to the First Law of Thermodynamics, we know that energy cannot be created nor destroyed. Furthermore, the work of Steven Hawking validated that even if the information meets the event horizon of a black hole, the information with not be destroyed; rather, it is stored in a 2D hologram.[20]

Jay Baer is correct, *"we're surrounded by data, but starved for insights."* I believe one day soon, science will validate the process of accessing all the data that surrounds us. You might even find a way before then. However, until then, keep chopping wood and carrying water.

Chapter 9

Skills Are Like Tools. They Work Best When Sharpened.

"Unless you are continually improving your skills, you're quickly becoming irrelevant."

—Stephen R. Covey-

Are you impatient? I know I can be, although nothing like I used to be. Embarrassingly, at one time, I was the biggest offender. Yes, shamefully so, and even at times obnoxiously!

I could not wait in line for anything. I would pay every maître d to get a table faster, the door attendant to sidestep the crowd, and even buy people coffee if I could shortcut the line. One time I even purchased a woman's groceries because she was fumbling through her wallet for money and coming up short, so I gave out enough money to pay for the lady's weekly groceries.

On another occasion, I departed my home in Los Angeles to travel to Paris to meet friends for a two-week vacation. I was super excited to go to France and be with friends and attend the 24 Hours of Le Mans car race. Just the idea of all the high-end exotic cars speeding around the irregular course with fans from across the globe was exhilarating.

The adrenaline was high as I arrived at Los Angeles International Airport. To my surprise, the check-in line stretched to the next terminal. There were hundreds of people, and I was in absolute shock. I could feel the adrenaline shift.

I had enough time to wait in line and get on the plane. However, it did not matter. Instead of exercising patience, I opted for stupidity and entered the Business Class check-in line to shortcut the process. They quickly laid it on me. "I am afraid we have no Business Class seats available, so your only option, Sir, is to wait in line and hope you make the flight." Unacceptable!

The impatience skyrocketed along with my anxiety, and before I knew it, I purchased a $12,000 first-class ticket in addition to the other ticket I already was holding in my hand solely because I did not want to wait in line. Yes, for real!

To add to the stupidity, I got on the plane and popped an Ambien out of fear of not getting rest and being fresh upon arrival. Well, I did fall asleep for eleven hours, to be exact. I received a gentle wake-up shake from the flight attendant a mere twenty minutes prior to arrival. Brilliant! All I remember is the first thirty minutes of the flight and all for the economical price of $12,000.

Back then, I thought my skill was avoiding lines. I was a master at getting into any restaurant, club, concert, or any other event for that matter without reservation or incident, as if I were a celebrity. What made matters worse was that my family and friends knew how talented I was in this regard and was always ready, willing, and able to put me to the test.

Yes, I have many eccentric and ridiculous memories to share from this wonderful skill I developed. However, what I really did was deny myself the opportunity to exercise patience, real skill, and talent. A skill that I should have developed sooner. Because I denied myself the opportunity to have more meaningful moments. I suppose we all live and learn at our own pace.

Over time I learned to refrain from carelessly distributing cash to everyone. More importantly, I began to focus on developing the skills that would better serve me moving forward. For instance, I made the effort to be mindful of my other unpleasant habits to improve my behavior and improve the quality of my life. I learned to be present, connect with people on a personal level, and create meaningful and lasting relationships without all the stupidity.

We all possess skills that are more than sufficient for us to reach our goals and live a happy life. If we want to achieve those goals and live a happy and rewarding life, then we need to be aware of those skills and how to develop them. We also need to be aware of the challenges we may face along the way. Even your greatest challenge, which we will discuss later in the book.

Skills are broken down into two categories: Hard Skills & Soft Skills.

Hard Skills are technical knowledge or training you gain through life experience that includes your education and career. We may also develop these skills through other avenues, such as pursuing hobbies or interests related to those skills. Some examples of Hard Skills are interior design, acting, cinematography, auto servicing, software development, plumbing, and data entry.

In contrast, Soft Skills are personal habits and traits that shape how you work on your own and with others. They are also known as soft or people skills.

Some Soft Skills are critical thinking, empathy, open-mindedness, teamwork, creativity, adaptability, problem-solving, and integrity.

You may want to sit down and compile a list of both the hard and soft skills you possess. If you have a resume, I hope you have done it. If you have not, you should for potential employment and, more importantly, for yourself.

Employers initially focus on your hard and soft skills when they consider you for a position. Enumerating your hard and soft skills and highlighting the work you have accomplished demonstrates how you have managed to capitalize on your talents. It also hints at your future potential. I highly recommend adding both skill sets to your resume.

Personally, the benefits of listing and evaluating your skills are incalculable.

However, to receive those benefits, you will need to do some work. In a previous chapter, we discussed techniques to help you achieve your goals. One that would be of particular benefit in your quest is the SWOT Analysis. It is fast, precise, and actionable.

I recommend you first list the hard skills in one column and then the soft skills in a second column. You can do this exercise on a piece of paper or your computer on Word, Excel, or another program you feel comfortable with. I like to use Excel because I can easily move content around. You will understand shortly.

The following step is particularly important. Remember, soft skills include habits and traits, both good and bad. You would not list the negative ones on your resume, but addressing them for your benefit will be beneficial and rewarding, so list them in the column.

Now, on a separate piece of paper or the same Excel sheet, create four columns or sections. Label the sections Strengths, Weaknesses, Opportunities, and Weakness. Start populating each section with the Hard Skills only. Do not give too much thought to where to place each hard skill. Place each one where you initially sense it belongs.

Note that it is not imperative to have the same number of entries in each column. In other words, you need not have four hard skills in each column. Similarly, you need not have four soft skills in each column.

It would be highly unusual if that is the case. You will have more hard and soft skills in the Strengths column and less in the Threats column. It is normal, so do not worry about it.

Having completed the hard skill placement segment, stop and walk away without reviewing your work for an hour or so. Do you have errands, or can you listen to music? Whatever the case may be, take a break and come back in an hour or more.

Welcome back! Now, look over your work without judgment. Does anything feel out of place? In other words, do you feel you properly categorized your hard skills?

If the answer is no, which is quite possible, then create another piece of paper and list the misplaced hard skills in it. Do not change your original work! Simply list the misplaced habits and traits on the new piece of paper under the heading you now believe they should appear. Leave room for commentary on each of these skills, something you will do later.

It is now time to return to your original SWOT analysis. As I previously said, do not alter any of your previous work. You will now add your soft skills to the same columns. Continue down each column by adding habits and traits as you feel fit. Again, I recommend you do it quickly and with truly little thought. Once you complete the task, immediately walk away for at least an hour.

Terrific! Excellent work if you have followed the directions and have completed these steps. I know it may seem like a considerable amount of work. However, I promise you the benefits are huge and immediate.

Hopefully, you enjoyed your break. Now let us get back to it. You may now review your SWOT analysis that contains both your hard and soft skills.

Do you notice anything interesting? Do you notice how you perceive yourself? Do you tend to see yourself with strengths, few weaknesses, or vice versa? Do you see yourself as a fearful person with threats?

The SWOT analysis brings more to light than just arranging hard and soft skills in columns. Hopefully, it reveals more to you about who you are and your behaviors. Importantly, write down your new revelations and anything else that comes to mind.

You may now shift around the soft skills if you feel compelled. Once you are satisfied, it is time to return to the piece of paper or Excel section where you have recategorized your hard skills. Review your choices, and then next to each one, write an explanation as to why you moved it in the first place. If, after writing your explanation, you feel your initial choice was incorrect, you may now adjust the skill on your master SWOT sheet.

Keep all your work handy. You will need it for reference in the next and last steps. Be mindful that the work you have now completed has placed your hard and soft skills at the center of your awareness. You now sit with the opportunity to improve your talents, habits, traits, yourself, and chances of succeeding.

The last step in the process is to create a separate sheet to write down empowering statements based on your observations. These statements are also known as Affirmations. I highly recommend pen and paper versus Microsoft Word or another computer program. The reason is it is scientifically proven that hand-written notes have a reinforcing effect on the brain.

In other words, the sensation of pen on paper creates stimuli that reinforce the experience, making it easier to remember the information. You may then apply the techniques you learned to supercharge your skills. You will also find the experience empowering.

To start, keep in mind that the purpose of this step is to create positive and powerful statements that will reinforce your thoughts. In other words, you will create affirmations that will encourage you, give you confidence, reduce and hopefully eliminate doubt and unhealthy habits, and prompt you to take the act with confidence.

Before you commence, take time to get relaxed and comfortable. If you do not, it will be more difficult to formulate the affirmations, and they may not be concise. The more concise the statements are, the better results you will achieve, so do not cheat yourself by rushing. Do breathing exercises, take a walk, or do whatever you need to do to get relaxed.

Ready? The following are the basic rules you need to know to get started.

1. All affirmations should begin with either the word I or My.
2. Short affirmations are the easiest to remember.
   Example: I am a kind person.
3. Affirmations are always positive statements.
   Example: I can achieve even difficult tasks.
4. Write them in the present tense as if you are experiencing them now.
   Example: I see I am wealthy in all ways.
5. Only write statements that you believe are possible.
6. Include an emotion.
   Positive emotions are a trigger for positive action.
   Example: I am thankful for everything in my life.
7. The statements should be written as if you have already achieved what you seek.
   Example: I am wealthy and excited for more wealth on its way.

Don'ts:

1. Never use negative words
2. Never use the past tense
3. Never use dates or exact amounts; they are limiting.
4. Never say I want or need. Focus on what you have and will realize.

You now have the basics to get going. However, I highly encourage you to research affirmations on your own for two reasons. One, the research will reinforce the information I am sharing. Two, you will receive more examples that will help you formulate affirmations for the specific things you seek.

Once you compile your list of affirmations, I encourage you to write them neatly on a notepad with a pen and keep them next to your bed. Read them every day, at least at night before you go to bed or first thing in the morning.

For best results, read them in the morning and evening. Importantly, be sure you are in a relaxed state when you read them. Simply reading the words with not produce the best results. The more present you are and the more you feel the emotion in each statement, the more it will resonate and the more confidence you will feel as you work to achieve a goal.

In conclusion, skills are like tools. They work best when sharpened. Using a SWOT analysis, you now have a methodology to help you detect and better understand your hard and soft skills. You can focus on improving your strengths and eliminating the things that do not serve your best interests. Mastering your hard and soft skills will position you to capitalize on more opportunities and achieve better results.

I am excited for you because your demanding work is already paying off. If you do not see the benefits quite yet, be patient, you will shortly. Congratulations, you are well on your way to achieving the success you desire and deserve. Well done!

Chapter 10

Life Is More Enjoyable Having Positive Experiences.

"A positive mindset brings positive things."

—Philipp Reiter-

Obviously, no? But why is life more enjoyable than having positive experiences? Ever thought about it? I am betting if you have thought about it, it is not to any great degree! Is it genuinely worth examining this question, and if so, to what degree? You may or may not be surprised by the answer, but either way, you will receive a benefit that makes it well worth reading.

Because by the end of this chapter, you will understand why these questions are so important. You will also harness the power of the answers to improve your experiences as you progress forward to achieve the meaningful things you desire. Most importantly, you will enjoy the process and realize your desires with less effort and friction.

The science on this matter is quite straightforward. Five main chemicals in the human body are responsible for happiness. They are dopamine, endorphin, serotonin, oxytocin, and cortisol. Each one has a different and notable effect on our brain and behavior. Understanding how each one affects us is an opportunity to improve our mental state, productivity, and chances of achieving our dreams.

Dopamine is widely known for the role it plays in the reward system of our brain. If we do something which our brain finds rewarding, we then receive a shot of dopamine. The reason for the surge is to remember the positive action and encourage us to do it again.

Researchers suspected that dopamine might play a role in influencing how the brain evaluates whether a mental task is worth the effort. The team, co-led by Dr. Michael Frank from Brown University, performed experiments to assess dopamine's role in motivation. The study was funded in part by NIH's National Institute of Mental Health (NIMH). The findings appeared in *Science* on March 20, 2020.

Fifty people, ages 18 to 43, participated in the study. The scientists first measured the levels of natural dopamine in the participant's striatum. Participants were asked to choose between a series of memory tasks of varying difficulties. More difficult mental tasks were rewarded with more money.

The team found that those with higher dopamine levels in a region of the striatum called the caudate nucleus were more likely to focus on the benefits (the money) and choose the difficult mental tasks. Those with lower dopamine levels were more sensitive to the perceived cost or task difficulty.

The participants then completed experiments after taking an inactive placebo, methylphenidate, or sulpiride—an antipsychotic medication that, at low doses, increases dopamine levels. Increasing dopamine boosted how willing people with low, but not high, dopamine synthesis capacity in the caudate nucleus were to choose more difficult mental tasks. It did this by changing its cost/benefit sensitivity. The results from these experiments reflected the findings for naturally varying dopamine levels.[21]

In short, endorphin is considered a natural painkiller. I am sure you have heard of "runners high." It is when a runner passes a certain point of exertion, and they claim to experience a rush or euphoric feeling. What happens is the body releases endorphins when muscles are pushed near their limits to suppress the pain. However, most runners quickly forget the pain as they transition into a painless state. The transition is so significant that they often describe the transition as a high. Meaning catapulted into a happier physical and mental state.

Of course, once the endorphin leaves our body, we start to feel muscle pain. However, most people describe the pain as a positive pain resulting in our physical growth and development.

People have long associated exercise with endorphins, even without being aware of the science behind it.

There is science, however.

For example, a 2018 meta-analysis shows an association between resistance exercise training and a significant reduction in depressive symptoms. The researchers found that this effect occurred regardless of a person's health status, the amount of resistance exercise they took part in, or whether they saw any significant improvements in physical strength.

Likewise, a 2019 meta-analysis suggests that performing 45 minutes of moderate-intensity aerobic exercise three times per week can have a significant antidepressant effect.

Other physical activities, including dancing and having sex, can also boost endorphin levels. The well-known "runner's high" that people experience after lengthy, vigorous exercise is also due to an increase in endorphin levels.

Because of this evidence, it is unusual for doctors to prescribe exercise alongside therapy or medication for treating depressive symptoms.

Increasing the body's natural endorphin levels may be an effective way for a person to improve their overall health.

Although research is ongoing, scientists have found that higher endorphin levels can reduce pain and increase pleasure. High endorphin levels may also help:

- reduce symptoms of stress, anxiety, and depression
- improve moods
- boost self-esteem
- support cognitive function
- promote immune system health
- reduce inflammation
- regulate appetite

Endorphin levels and the stimuli that help increase them may vary from person to person. So far, research seems to emphasize that physical activity, certain foods, and various enjoyable activities boost endorphin levels.

While health professionals accept that eating palatable foods can boost people's endorphin levels, research has focused on more specific categories.

For example, studies suggest that eating dark chocolate rich in cocoa — ideally 70% cocoa or higher — can boost levels of endorphins and dopamine. Dopamine is another feel-good brain chemical.

Additionally, research has shown a link between eating spicy foods and a spike in endorphin levels. The theory is that the body produces endorphins to counteract the pain of the food's burning sensation.

Research has investigated the perceived health benefits of laughter. Laughing can increase endorphin levels and have other positive effects on the body.

For example, a 2019 meta-analysis found that laughter may improve anxiety and depression symptoms and sleep quality.

Another 2019 review makes a case for further research into the link between pain and humor.

A person can bring more laughter and humor into their lives in many ways, such as by spending time with friends or family.

Some research suggests a potential link between low endorphin levels and certain health conditions or symptoms.

When a person's body does not produce enough endorphins, they may be at an increased risk of:

- unintentional weight loss
- body aches and pains
- depression and anxiety
- moodiness
- trouble sleeping
- addiction

Research on the link between health conditions and endorphins is ongoing. For example, one study found that increases in the body's endorphins were correlated with pain relief in people with fibromyalgia.

Endorphins are a type of brain chemical that helps people cope with pain and stress.

Healthy levels of endorphins can help people deal with physical pain, moodiness, and symptoms of anxiety or depression. Low endorphin levels may increase a person's risk of body aches and pains, sleep difficulties, and addiction.

Scientists' understanding of human endorphin levels is still evolving. Researchers believe that people can increase levels of this feel-good chemical through activities such as exercising, eating endorphin-releasing foods like dark chocolate, and tapping into their sense of humor.[22]

Next up is Oxytocin. It is the chemical responsible for social bonding. I find Oxytocin quite interesting because this chemical has an effect that extends beyond our bodies. What happens is when you have any positive interactions with other people, it causes a surge of oxytocin. The result is we want to spend more time with these people. It also occurs when we interact with animals, such as pets, and explains why pet owners report a better sense of well-being when they are with their pets.

Oxytocin is more than a fleeting chemical high. It is a hormone that functions as a neurotransmitter in the brain. It is thought to be a driving force behind attraction and caregiving and even controls key aspects of the reproductive system, childbirth, and lactation.

Oxytocin has earned the nickname "the cuddle" or "love" hormone because it's released when people snuggle up, have sex, or bond socially—in fact, the effect is so strong that even petting a dog has been shown to release it. Yet recent findings have shed new light on the effects of oxytocin and why it may not be all kisses and hugs.

Robert C. Froemke, Ph.D., a neuroscientist who studies oxytocin at New York University, concurs. "Oxytocin is not a 'trust hormone' or 'love drug'—there is no such thing, biologically speaking. Oxytocin is released during social contact and gaze, mother-infant bonding, and birthing, and in other cases as well," he explains. "Most current neuroscientific studies of oxytocin indicate that oxytocin doesn't always make people happier or more pro-social or willing to bond. Rather, oxytocin seems to act like a volume dial, turning up and amplifying brain activity related to whatever someone is already experiencing. That's essentially what a lot of different recent studies are converging on for oxytocin."

Despite these mixed signals, oxytocin plays an undeniably vital role in establishing and maintaining relationships. And it all begins in one place: the brain. Once oxytocin is produced by the hypothalamus, a portion of the brain that keeps the body's internal functions in balance, it is secreted into the bloodstream by the pituitary gland. From there, oxytocin is directed into your spinal cord or other parts of the brain, depending on its ultimate purpose.

Released into our brains under the right circumstances, oxytocin has the power to regulate our emotional responses and pro-social behaviors, including trust, empathy, gazing, positive memories, processing of bonding cues, and positive communication. Thanks to oxytocin, we get a toasty, tranquil feeling whenever we are with the people we care about. And the more we engage in these feel-good behaviors, the more oxytocin we get—you might even call it addictive.

Oxytocin is also connected to serotonin and dopamine. This trio of neurotransmitters is often referred to as the "happy hormones," and for good reason. Under the right conditions, they work as a team to make us feel butterflies. Whenever we are with someone who we are attracted to or care about, our brain releases dopamine, serotonin levels increase, oxytocin is produced, and presto—you get the buzz that love songs are written about.

Releasing oxytocin requires one thing: another person. While it is traditionally associated with sex, breastfeeding, and childbirth, almost any form of social bonding or positive physical contact can trigger oxytocin. One study (on chimpanzees) even found that sharing a meal does the trick. Common triggers include:

- Positive physical contact (cuddling, kissing, hugging, holding hands)
- Social bonding (talking, making eye contact, laughing)

- Sex
- Breastfeeding
- Childbirth

Women typically have higher oxytocin levels than men. (It is a key hormone involved in childbirth and lactation, after all). Biological differences aside, men and women do share oxytocin experiences in the same ways. It facilitates bonding with children, increases romantic attachment, and plays a significant role in reproduction for both sexes.

Oxytocin is not all in your head. Here are additional ways it keeps our bodies running:

Calling oxytocin, the "love" hormone is a PG-rated version of the scientific truth. Oxytocin does not just induce cuddling—it plays a crucial role in the reproductive system itself. While the exact mechanism is not clear, sex has been found to stimulate the release of oxytocin, which intensify erection, ejaculation, and orgasms. Oxytocin also causes muscle contractions in the uterus and womb, which helps move sperm along and increases the chance of pregnancy.

Another trigger for oxytocin? Labor. As the cervix and vagina begin to widen for childbirth, oxytocin is released and starts a familiar feeling for mothers: contractions. This helps the baby move downward and out of the birth canal.

The connection between babies and oxytocin does not end there. Oxytocin stimulates the "let-down reflex" in breastfeeding, making it easier for milk to flow.

The effects of oxytocin on eating behavior and metabolism are increasingly being put under the microscope. A recent series of studies show that oxytocin reduces activity in the hypothalamus, an area of the brain that controls hunger, and increases activity in parts of the brain associated with impulse control.

When increased under stress-free conditions, some research (on rats) suggests that oxytocin promotes sleep by countering the effects of cortisol, a stress hormone. However, research in this area is limited.

The good news is: It is easy to raise your oxytocin levels—it all comes down to making social connections and bonds. You could get a massage. Listen to music. Give someone a hug. Or pet a dog (anyone will do). Influencing oxytocin levels artificially, however, is a bit more complicated. No food or over-the-counter medicines in the United States have been proven to increase oxytocin.[23]

Serotonin is a neurotransmitter that carries messages between nerve cells in your brain (your central nervous system) and throughout your body (your peripheral nervous system). These chemical messages tell your body how to work.

Serotonin plays a role in your body, including influencing learning, memory, and happiness, as well as regulating body temperature, sleep, sexual behavior, and hunger. Lack of enough serotonin is thought to play a role in depression, anxiety, mania, and other health conditions.

Serotonin is found in your gut (intestines). 90% of serotonin is found in the cells lining your gastrointestinal tract. It is released into your blood circulation and absorbed by platelets. Only about 10% is produced in your brain.

Serotonin is made from the essential amino acid tryptophan. An essential amino acid means it cannot be made by your body. It must be obtained from the foods you eat.

Serotonin plays a role in your body's functions:

- Mood: Serotonin in your brain regulates your mood. It is often called your body's natural "feel good" chemical. When serotonin is at normal levels, you feel more focused, emotionally stable, happier, and calmer. Low levels of serotonin are associated with depression. Medications used to treat anxiety, depression, and other mood disorders often target ways to increase the level of serotonin in your brain.

- Digestion: Your body's serotonin is in your GI tract, where it helps control your bowel function and plays a role in protecting your gut. Your gut can increase serotonin release to speed digestion to rid your body of irritating foods or toxic products. Serotonin also plays a part in reducing your appetite while eating.

- Nausea: Nausea is triggered when serotonin is released into your gut faster than it can be digested. The chemical message is received by your brain, which you perceive as nausea. Drugs used to reduce feelings of nausea and vomiting target specific serotonin receptors in your brain.

- Sleep: Serotonin, together with another neurotransmitter, dopamine, plays a role in the quality of your sleep (how well and how long you sleep). Your brain also needs serotonin to make melatonin, a hormone that regulates your sleep-wake cycle.

- Wound healing: Serotonin is released by platelets in your blood to help heal wounds. It also causes the tiniest blood vessels, arterioles, to narrow, which slows blood flow and helps clots to form. This is an important process in wound healing.

- Bone health: Serotonin levels may play a role in the density of your bones. High levels of serotonin in your gut may play a role in making bones weak, which can lead to bone breaks (fractures) and osteoporosis.

- Sexual health: Serotonin also plays a role — together with the neurotransmitter dopamine — in your desire for sex.

Low levels of serotonin may be associated with health conditions, including:

- Depression and other mood problems.
- Anxiety.
- Sleep problems.
- Digestive problems.
- Suicidal behavior.
- Obsessive-compulsive disorder.
- Post-traumatic stress disorder.
- Panic disorders.
- Schizophrenia.
- Phobias.

Scientists still have a lot to learn about the role of serotonin in the body and in disease.

A low serotonin level usually has more than one cause. Technically, serotonin levels are low because:

- Your body is not producing enough serotonin.
- Your body is not effectively using serotonin. This can happen if you do not have enough serotonin receptors or the receptors are not working as they should.

Ways to increase serotonin levels include:

- Eating more tryptophan-containing foods.
- Getting more sunlight.
- Taking certain supplements.
- Getting more exercise and lowering your stress level.

Many foods naturally contain tryptophan, the amino acid from which serotonin is made. You can try increasing your serotonin level by eating tryptophan-containing foods, such as:

- Salmon.
- Eggs.
- Cheese.
- Turkey.
- Tofu.
- Pineapples.
- Nuts, oats, and seeds.

Eating foods high in tryptophan will not necessarily boost serotonin levels on its own. It is a complex process. Your body needs carbohydrates to release insulin, which is needed to absorb amino acids. Then even if tryptophan does get into your blood, it has to compete with other amino acids to get absorbed into your brain. Scientists are still studying how eating tryptophan-containing foods boost serotonin levels.

Not getting enough exposure to sunlight can lead to the mood disorder seasonal affective disorder in some people. Try to get 10 to 15 minutes of sunlight each day to boost not only serotonin levels but vitamin D levels too. If you live in an area where you cannot get natural sunlight, consider using light therapy to get that needed daily sunlight.

Several dietary and herbal supplements also increase serotonin levels. These include:

- Dietary supplement: Tryptophan, probiotics, and SAMe.
- Herbal supplements: These can include ginseng, St. John's wort, Syrian rue, and nutmeg.

Regular exercise is known to increase serotonin levels. Thirty minutes of aerobic exercise five times a week plus two strength-training sessions per week can improve mood disorders and heart health.[24]

Last on the list is cortisol. I call it the antithesis chemical. We produce cortisol when we feel bad as a cue to address negative emotions. In other words, cortisol tells us to take action to counteract negative emotions. Ignoring the cues results in a release of even more cortisol and more negativity. Yes, cortisol is responsible for negativity, but it is essential to turn things around. Therefore. It plays a pivotal role in our happiness and well-being.

Cortisol is a glucocorticoid steroid hormone that your adrenal glands, the endocrine glands on top of your kidneys, produce and release. Cortisol affects several aspects of your body and helps regulate your body's response to stress.

Hormones are chemicals that coordinate contrasting functions in your body by carrying messages through your blood to your organs, skin, muscles, and other tissues. These signals tell your body what to do and when to do it.

Glucocorticoids are a type of steroid hormone that suppresses inflammation in all your bodily tissues and control metabolism in your muscles, fat, liver, and bones. Glucocorticoids also affect sleep-wake cycles.

Your adrenal glands, also known as suprarenal glands, are small, triangle-shaped glands that are located on top of each of your two kidneys. They're a part of your endocrine system.

Cortisol is an essential hormone that affects every organ and tissue in your body. It plays many important roles, including:

- Regulating your body's stress response.
- Helping control your body's use of fats, proteins, and carbohydrates, or your metabolism.
- Suppressing inflammation.
- Regulating blood pressure.
- Regulating blood sugar.
- Helping control your sleep-wake cycle.

Your body continuously monitors your cortisol levels to maintain steady levels (homeostasis). Higher-than-normal or lower-than-normal cortisol levels can be harmful to your health.

Cortisol is widely known as the "stress hormone." However, it has many important effects and functions throughout your body aside from regulating your body's stress response.

It is also important to remember that, biologically speaking, there are multiple various kinds of stress, including:

- Acute stress: Acute stress happens when you are in sudden danger within a brief period. For example, barely avoiding a car accident or being chased by an animal are situations that cause acute stress.
- Chronic stress: Chronic (long-term) stress happens when you experience ongoing situations that cause frustration or anxiety. For example, having a difficult or frustrating job or having a chronic illness can cause chronic stress.
- Traumatic stress: Traumatic stress happens when you experience a life-threatening event that induces fear and a feeling of helplessness. For example, experiencing an extreme weather event, such as a tornado, or experiencing war or sexual assault can cause traumatic stress. In some cases, these events can lead to post-traumatic stress disorder (PTSD).

Your body releases cortisol when you experience any of these types of stress.

All tissues in your body have glucocorticoid receptors. Because of this, cortisol can affect every organ system in your body, including:

- Nervous system.
- Immune system.
- Cardiovascular system.
- Respiratory system.

- Reproductive systems (female and male).
- Musculoskeletal system.
- Integumentary system (skin, hair, nails, glands, and nerves).

More specifically, cortisol affects your body in the following ways:

- Regulating your body's stress response: During times of stress, your body can release cortisol after releasing its "fight or flight" hormones, such as adrenaline, so you continue to stay on high alert. In addition, cortisol triggers the release of glucose (sugar) from your liver for fast energy during times of stress.
- Regulating metabolism: Cortisol helps control how your body uses fats, proteins, and carbohydrates for energy.
- Suppressing inflammation: In short spurts, cortisol can boost your immunity by limiting inflammation. However, if you have consistently elevated levels of cortisol, your body can get used to having too much cortisol in your blood, which can lead to inflammation and a weakened immune system.
- Regulating blood pressure: The exact way in which cortisol regulates blood pressure in humans is unclear. However, elevated levels of cortisol can cause high blood pressure, and lower-than-normal levels of cortisol can cause low blood pressure.
- Increasing and regulating blood sugar: Under normal circumstances, cortisol counterbalances the effect of insulin, a hormone your pancreas makes, to regulate your blood sugar. Cortisol raises blood sugar by releasing stored glucose, while insulin lowers blood sugar. Having chronically high cortisol levels can lead to persistent high blood sugar (hyperglycemia). This can cause Type 2 diabetes.
- Helping control your sleep-wake cycle: Under regular circumstances, you have lower cortisol levels in the evening

when you go to sleep and peak levels in the morning right before you wake up. This suggests that cortisol plays a significant role in the initiation of wakefulness and plays a part in your body's circadian rhythm.

Your body has an elaborate system to regulate your cortisol levels.

Your hypothalamus, a small area of your brain involved in hormonal regulation, and your pituitary gland, a tiny gland located below your brain, regulate the production of cortisol in your adrenal glands. When the levels of cortisol in your blood fall, your hypothalamus releases corticotropin-releasing hormone (CRH), which directs your pituitary gland to produce adrenocorticotropic hormone (ACTH). ACTH then stimulates your adrenal glands to produce and release cortisol.

To have optimal levels of cortisol in your body, your hypothalamus, pituitary gland, and adrenal glands must all be functioning properly.

In general, though, there are several everyday things you can do to try to lower your cortisol levels and keep them at optimal ranges, including:

- Get quality sleep: Chronic sleep issues, such as obstructive sleep apnea, insomnia, or working a night shift, are associated with higher cortisol levels.
- Exercise regularly: Several studies have shown that regular exercise helps improve sleep quality and reduce stress, which can help lower cortisol levels over time.
- Learn to limit stress and stressful thinking patterns: Being aware of your thinking pattern, breathing, heart rate, and other signs of tension help you recognize stress when it begins and can help you prevent it from becoming worse.

- ☼ Practice deep breathing exercises: Controlled breathing helps stimulate your parasympathetic nervous system, your "rest and digest" system, which helps lower cortisol levels.

- ☼ Enjoy yourself and laugh: Laughing promotes the release of endorphins and suppresses cortisol. Participating in hobbies and fun activities can also promote feelings of well-being, which may lower your cortisol levels.

- ☼ Maintain healthy relationships: Relationships are a significant aspect of our lives. Having tense and unhealthy relationships with loved ones or coworkers can cause frequent stress and raise your cortisol levels.

Cortisol is an essential hormone that impacts several aspects of your body. While there are several things you can do to try to limit your stress and therefore manage your cortisol levels, sometimes having abnormally high or low levels of cortisol is out of your control.[27]

As you can see, everyone has chemicals within them that affect their physical and mental well-being. Paying attention to the cues that are produced is an opportunity to re-evaluate and rebalance yourself to have more positive experiences. With greater awareness and a healthier lifestyle, you can dramatically improve your mood, experiences, focus, productivity, and chances of success.

Chapter 11

The Primary Benefit Of Working With Others Is Not Achieving A Common Goal.

"Nothing is more expensive than a missed opportunity."

—H. Jackson Brown Jr.-

It was the 1960s. A transformative time in history, with polarizing movements on the rise and monumental events taking place frequently. Many became indelible moments in human history.

There was the Vietnam War, The Civil Rights Movement, Political Assassinations, Free Love, and more. There is one of the most revolutionary moments in human history. I am talking about the Moon Landing on July 20, 1969.

I was just a kid at the time on a family vacation visiting my grandparents in Miami, Florida. It may be hard to believe, but I remember it clearer than yesterday.

I recall the room we sat in and every detail about it with flawless clarity. The long gold couch with four distinct pillow sections. Each pillow was outlined in piping. The couch sat between two gold upholstered wood end chairs. The chairs had dark wood pedestal legs, each leg with vertical inscriptions around the entire leg. The chair's arms were carved as well and contoured like waves to accommodate the perfect armrest position. The back of the chairs wrapped around in an outline of burled dark wood with cushiony gold upholstered backs.

The wood coffee table had burled legs and a glass insert top, the lamps had a square wood base and rectangular post that rose to a beige lampshade, and the pictures on the wall were those painted by my grandmother, who was an artist, and of course, the black and white TV encased in a mid-tone wood cabinet positioned across the far wall with my grandmother's sacred phonograph also encased in a similar wood cabinet sitting adjacent.

It is remarkable to me how much that event played in my memory. I remember anxiously awaiting and vacillating between doubt, if it was even possible, and goosebumps of excitement. It was surreal, and as we waited, each family member would chime in and share a thought or a feeling.

My point is that there are moments that are monumental. They are the culmination of countless peoples' efforts to accomplish a common goal. A goal that is considered the pinnacle. However, for those associated with such projects, the primary benefit of working with others is not achieving the pinnacle or common goal.

Why? Because reaching the goal is one thing, and once it is, what is next? The pinnacle has passed, like the exit on a freeway, and onward we go. Tomorrow comes, and it is a new day! We live in the present and look toward the future.

If you choose to work with others for the primary benefit of achieving a common goal, I promise you will sadly be disappointed. It

Consider this?!

is easy to adopt such a perspective because that is the pep talk others use to sell us their dream.

There is nothing wrong with joining a worthy project, and I highly encourage you to do so. What I suggest is you be clear on the real benefits you will receive because once you do achieve the goal and the party is over, you will be staring squarely into a new day, feeling like a void.

The following story related to the famous Moon Landing will put things into perspective. Leading up to the Moon Landing, President John F. Kennedy was passing through the halls of the NASA Space Center in Houston. He paused for a few moments to talk to the janitor, who was holding a broom.

President Kennedy introduced himself in his typical yet distinctive manner. "Hi, I'm Jack…." And he proceeded to ask the janitor what he was doing. The janitor responded, "I'm helping put a man on the moon." He saw his job as more than just sweeping floors. He perceived it as playing a role in putting a man on the moon and a giant leap for humankind.

In other words, the janitor felt empowered, which is terrific, and he should! However, how about the day after the moon Landing? Sure, the janitor could claim bragging rights. But it is always a new day, a new pinnacle to reach, and the gas in the tank only lasts so long. Others are only impressed for so long.

Now that the event occurred, what real benefit does the janitor have left? Should the janitor's goal be sweeping the floors to help put a man on the moon? By helping to put a man on the moon, did the janitor improve his sweeping abilities? These are all valid and important questions to ask. One should be clear on why they are doing what they set out to do.

The average person spends an average of up to 90,000+ hours or a third of their life working. It is difficult to experience fulfillment for the rest of your life if you are hesitant to go to work every day. You need to be clear on what benefits you will receive and how they will improve your life, not just your career.

The obvious thing is to find more meaningful work. I mean finding work with a clear purpose. It is well documented that people who work for not-for-profit organizations and social enterprises are much more satisfied with their jobs and happier with their lives. Also, social sciences demonstrate, categorically, that the meaning we find in our work is from what we glean from the experiences we have and has less to do with the tasks themselves.

People may or may not agree with my comment that the primary benefit of working with others is not achieving a common goal. Case in point, I recently floated the comment by an acquaintance on a trip to Miami. Their immediate response was with a smug bitter face, "who even cares? The only reason to work is to make money. That is the only goal!" I was not surprised by the response or even phased by the fact the comment came from a Wharton MBA graduate.

Having observed this person for several years, it was apparent that their everyday existence of chasing money with the information they learned in school has yet to deliver the financial rewards they wished for or, more importantly, any happiness. They rarely smile, laugh, spend time building meaningful personal relationships or share anything of value with anyone.

In other words, they live a life of isolation placing money at the pinnacle. They spend their time sucking up to the people they work with in hopes their colleagues will deliver them the fortune to solve all their problems.

However, it is more than a decade later, and fortune has yet to arrive. More importantly, their existence is no better than when they started. Still, they cling to their coveted Wharton degree as the golden ticket to happiness. Sadly, if they are fortunate enough to realize the financial payoff, it will lead to the realization that it came at far too great of a cost.

Consider this?!

Another person who bought into the great illusion that education will lead to money that will solve all the problems. Again, half of what we learn is false, and here is another example. If only this person had learned of the five greatest things of value, they would have known that money is at the bottom and information is next in line. Something you will not learn at Wharton or any other business school because it takes the focus off their curriculum and what is of most value in life.

If you want to see the value of an MBA degree, let us put it into perspective. How many of the most successful business people in the world have an MBA from Wharton? Take your best guess! Now tell me how many of these people have an MBA degree, including those from Wharton.

The following are presently the ten richest men in the world and their college education.

1. Elon Musk attended Queens University in Ontario, Canada, before transferring to the University of Pennsylvania.
2. Jeff Bezos attended Princeton University
3. Bernard Arnault attended École Polytechnique, Palaiseau,
4. Bill Gates attended Harvard University and dropped out,
5. Larry Page University of Michigan (BS) and Stanford University (MS)
6. Warren Buffet attended Wharton Business School for two years and then transferred and graduated from the University of Nebraska with a BA in Business Administration. He then received a Master's in Economics from Columbia University
7. Sergey Brin attended the University of Maryland, College Park (BS), and then Stanford University (MS)
8. Steve Balmer attended Harvard University (BA)
9. Larry Ellison attended the University of Illinois, Urbana-Champaign (no degree) · University of Chicago (no degree)

10. <u>Mukesh Ambani</u> attended St. Xavier's College, Mumbai · Institute of Chemical Technology (B.E.) · Stanford University (drop-out)

How did you do? What did you notice? Surprised? Yes, not one single person on the list has an MBA from Wharton .... or any other university! Some of the most financially successful men dropped out of college.

Yes, it is good to receive an education! However, the value is not in the information you receive while attending. The information is merely a bridge to the next greatest thing of value. And guess what? That information is available everywhere, not only at the most touted centers for education. It explains how the ten richest men rose to the top of financial fortune without the benefit of a fancy diploma.

As an observation, not everyone is determined to have a wealthy life. A deeply meaningful life filled with positivity, wonder, excitement, success, and happiness is more important.

People are often satisfied living a limiting life focused on the illusion that money will cure all and satisfy their ego that they achieved success and even happiness. They experience their share of lows with few, if any, highs. There is little to no personal growth and minimal success, and they realize little of themselves, and that is perfectly fine. As they say, "different strokes for different folks." Or "that is what makes it a horse race."

In any event, I know that it is not you. You are perfectly fine with a burger or pizza and yet, want something more eclectic, exotic, or upscale. You like more than one genre or two of music. Superficial conversations about where you went on your trip and what you ate are only the tip of the conversation. Knowing the details and the sensory experience is where the richness lies, and you want it.

Things are not black and white to you. There are plenty shades of grey, and you can appreciate many, if not all, of them. You see, tomorrow offers promise, and you look forward to meeting it head-

Consider this?!

on with positivity and even a smile. And I want to see you experience exactly that.

Understanding why the primary benefit of working with others is not achieving a common goal, such as financial rewards, is powerful. Learning the true benefit of why we should work with others is equally powerful. You will find it empowering and motivating, and it will keep you focused so you may achieve that which you desire. And you are now closer to realizing it.

So, why do we work with others if it is not primarily to achieve a common goal? It is easier if we start by asking why we work together in the first place. These answers are more obvious. For instance, we need a job to pay our bills, and part of that job is working with others to achieve a common goal. There, the question is answered so we can make money. Lol. Sure, I suppose so but is it that simple?

Let us say you are offered $100,000 to work with a group of four people for roughly a few hours. All you are asked to complete is a simple task. The task is to push a stalled Jeep through the basin of the jungle for a mile to the main road, where you will be met by a flatbed trailer that will take the vehicle to be repaired. Easy enough?

Sure, no problem! Oh, the path that you and your team will pass is covered with snakes of all sizes. And you will be given nothing to address this challenge. Still up for the task? You will receive $100,000.

If you are like most people, the answer will be an emphatic no. However, not everyone would answer no. And it is not because they are not afraid. They are willing to go through the experience to get the reward because they know they will gain something more valuable than money.

In other words, it is a challenge they are willing to take because what they will receive, if successful, is equally valuable, if not more than the money. Care to guess what is more valuable than money?

Put the fear aside for a moment and think about it. If the roadway was clear and it was a matter of collectively exerting physical force to get the vehicle to the roadway, you may say, sure, I will give it a try. And, if you and the team succeeded, you would get your financial reward.

Now, tell me how you think you would feel in that moment, knowing you did it. Would you experience satisfaction, elevated confidence, joy, happiness, or even bliss? How much value would be in that accomplishment? Do you think you would continue to experience those feelings once the money was spent?

That is why you will need to accomplish the task with the challenge I first presented. Now you must face your fear, see what you are made of, and decide if you are up for the challenge. And if you say yes? And if you succeed? How much value will the experience hold for you? Is it worth less than $100,000, the same or more? In any event, I am sure you will agree it is worth more than simply pushing the vehicle through the jungle with no snakes in your way.

In the above example, what is the challenge? Is it pushing the jeep, or is it contending with the snakes? Contending with the snakes. It is a mental challenge, not a physical challenge, and knowing you can overcome your doubts and fears is of far greater value because it will affect how you move forward in your life. In contrast, getting the $100,000 may affect your life in the near term, but the effect will not outlast the knowledge and wisdom you gained from the experience.

How about a real-life example? Yes, one of the richest people in the entire world could not make any money at first. Bill Gates' first company, Traf-O-Data (a device that could read traffic tapes and process the data), failed miserably. When Bill and his partner, Paul Allen, tried to sell it, the product did not even work. However, Bill and Paul did not let it stand in their way of success. When asked in an interview, Paul Allen explained that the failure helped them: "Even though Traf-O-Data wasn't a roaring success, it was seminal in preparing us to make Microsoft's first product a couple of years later."

Consider this?!

The knowledge gained was invaluable because it led to the two of them becoming the richest men in the world, even decades later.

Did you know one of the most frequent questions asked in a job interview is to describe a challenge you faced and how you overcame it? Employers know the value of people willing to take on a challenge, people that are not afraid to fail because they understand the value in what they will learn from the experience and people that will go the extra mile to reach the goal.

The next time you are presented with the opportunity to work with others for a common outcome, consider your motivation. Why is questioning your motivation a good question to ask yourself?

As I discuss in detail in my previous book, motivation is a key component to achieving success. There are two types of motivation. We touched on them in my previous example of pushing the Jeep through the jungle.

First, there is External Motivation. As it implies, it is when you are motivated by some external force. For example, a reward of some sort, such as money. In Pavlov's experiments, it was the food.

External motivation can be an effective tool at times. I will give you a quick example. Many years ago, I was rollerblading with my two sons, who were seven and eight at the time. We were in Aspen, Colorado, on the Rio Grande Trail. The trail is 42 miles long and runs from Aspen to Glenwood Springs.

We were around 10 miles from home, and my younger son declared he was exhausted and needed to rest. We stopped and rested for a while, and then he declared he was unable to skate back home. Unfortunately, the trail is in the woods, and the Roaring Fork River divides the trail from any access to the road, which is quite far from the river.

In other words, the only way home was to skate. Knowing my son has a weakness for ice cream, I told him that if he skated at least back to town, I would buy him the biggest ice cream sundae he could eat at Boogie's Diner. It was his favorite food at his favorite restaurant and hard to turn down.

His eyes lit up, but he still doubted he could make the trek. I suggested we try to skate back slowly and rest as often as needed. We began skating, and all my older son and I talked about was how great it was going to be to have a sundae at Boogie's. We mentioned the various flavors, combinations of sundaes, and other tasty treats at Boogie's. As I am sure you can guess, we eventually made it Boogie's.

Now, instead of the sundae at Boogie's, I offered him a chicken sandwich. We would not have made it a mile let alone 10. The point is that the food was the external motivation. And it needed to be enough to get the desired result. We also implemented visualization to keep him focused.

Sometimes, the reward is insufficient. For instance, had he been alone with no one talking to him and coaxing him along, he may have given up. Commonly, external motivation fails because people re-evaluate along the way and decide the reward is not sufficient for the effort.

On the other hand, we have Internal Motivation. Internal motivation is a much more powerful force and comes from within oneself. Using the same example, if my son feared we were vulnerable to attack by wild animals with self-preservation on his mind, his level of motivation would far out way his motivation for an ice cream sundae.

Tapping into your motivation is powerful. It is an invaluable tool for understanding. It provides clarity that will increase your chances of success. It is always beneficial to question your motivation before entering any venture.

Even more powerful than motivation is purpose. Similar to motivation, if your purpose is not in alignment with the tasks before you, then the likelihood you will finish or produce quality results remains low. Therefore, when considering joining a group project, always consider whether your purpose and motivation are in alignment with the project.

I implore you to remember that the primary benefit of working with others is to achieve something greater than yourself. Always keep in mind your motivation, purpose, and the benefits you stand to achieve. When you do meet a project that aligns with your purpose and motivation, you will experience elevated mental states, greater opportunities, positive reinforcement, as well as considerable and invaluable personal growth. Aren't these things important to you?

Chapter 12

An Instant Of Change Can Transform A Life Forever.

"Change is hard at first, messy in the middle and gorgeous at the end."

—Robin Sharma-

In the instant of a moment, a diagnosis was delivered, and a death sentence was handed down! "I'm terribly sorry to say you are looking at perhaps four months to live," the doctor said. I will never forget those words.

I was blown away! Shock! Grief! Anxiety!

A sinking wave-like feeling straight to my stomach, dizziness, and the intense urge to vomit! I saw the floor before me and almost hit it. Yet, I was able to reach the adjacent desk to catch my fall. Otherwise, I would have most certainly met it face first.

Why? How could this be? Why was it not noticed sooner? How could this have happened? Is this even really happening? WTF? What can I do?

Why, why, why? The questions reeled through my mind at light speed. Nothing made any sense! Except, numb!

The doctor continued, "it is a rare form of cancer. A cancer that is not only rare in infants but almost unheard of in adults. So rare that no research was being conducted to treat it. I am afraid there is nothing that can be done at this point."

It was everywhere. In the hip, all the back muscles up to the neck, and a tumor in the groin. The image of the x-ray was entirely black from the waste to the neck, and nothing could be done.

I experienced this nightmare with my son. He was 23 at the time. He was so heavily medicated he did not even react. I was not sure he knew they were talking to him instead of me. It seemed like many minutes went by until my son asked, "What do we do next?"

The doctor instructed us to visit the top oncologist at the most well-regarded cancer center in Seattle. "The oncologist will fill you in on the next steps when you get there." And so, we did. We got up, hailed a taxi, and sped off to see him. He was gracious enough to squeeze us into his busy schedule.

As one would expect from a doctor that sees death daily, he was very calm, cool, and collected. Our greeting was brief. He began reviewing the imaging and reports without missing a beat. We sat as he carefully scanned everything in front of us and then took a moment to gather his thoughts.

"I am terribly sorry to see you in this condition. There is nothing we can do to completely rid you of the cancer because of how it has spread. I recommend we perform surgery to remove it from the hip and some of the muscles, and I hope it buys you some time. "

"How much time?" my son asked.

"I am afraid I do not know. Perhaps several months more, but it is hard to say because the surgery will not stop the cancer, that we cannot extract," replied the doctor.

"What the fuck?" I thought.

"Doctor, you can explain to us what you have in mind?" I asked.

"Well, I would do a hip replacement, extract portions of the larger muscles, and try to scrape what I can from the remaining muscle tissue. Hopefully, with some chemotherapy, it will collectively buy you some more time. However, I must warn you that your ability to walk will be impaired due to the surgery. You may even require a wheelchair to get around."

"You must be fucking kidding me! Are you a sadist or what?" I did not say it, but I was thinking about it. I was fuming and about to explode. I caught myself, slid back into the chair, and then took a few deep breaths to collect myself.

My son jumped in, "what do I do next"? The doctor said, "you need the surgery. I want you to follow my nurse now to the operating room to get a port installed into your upper chest. You will need it for a variety of things, such as the chemotherapy and other fluids you will receive."

My son replied, "okay."

That was all I needed to hear. "Thank you, doctor, but it has been a long day, and my son needs rest. I will bring him back first thing in the morning, and they can install the port then." After significant resistance and a quick back and forth, the doctor agreed.

There must be an option! There must be an option! There must be an option! It was my mantra of the moment. Stop focusing on the problem and think of solutions. And, with that thought, that is exactly what I did. Immediately I felt compelled to get him back to Los Angeles for a second opinion.

We were both spent but were running out of time! I rushed my son to the airport and got on the first available flight. We got settled on the plane as the flight crew radioed ahead to make arrangements to greet us, and he passed out.

Again, the why questions began racing through my brain along with the adrenaline that was keeping me awake despite days of no sleep. The flight crew repeatedly consoled me as I struggled for a solution.

We eventually arrived and were shuttled off the plane directly to my car. It was a short but long night for me, and the morning came quickly. We arrived at Cedars Sinai at 7:00 am and met with the top cancer surgeon. An appointment I was able to arrange on our way to the Seattle airport the night before.

The surgeon told us that in cases like my son's, surgery is a failure 95% of the time, with the other 5% yielding minimal results. In his exact words, "if he were my son, I would absolutely not have surgery It is better he enjoys the remaining days 'as is' rather than enduring multiple surgeries and trying to recover from them with the eventual outcome the same. I'm terribly sorry, but I suggest you enjoy the following months!"

"If you change nothing, nothing will change."

– **Albert Einstein**

"Life will only change when you become more committed to your dreams than you are to your comfort zone."

- **Billy Cox**

"A wise man changes his mind, a fool never will."

– **Spanish proverb**

"Change the way you look at things and the things you look at change."

-**Wayne Dyer**

Consider this?!

"Those that cannot change their mind cannot change anything."

- George Bernard Shaw

"Insanity is doing the same thing over and over and expecting different results."

- Albert Einstein

An instant of change can transform a life forever. The concept is simple. Think about Marilyn Monroe, Robin Williams, Sylvia Plath, Kurt Cobain, Kate Spade, Anthony Bourdain, Avicii, Chris Cornell, Hunter S. Thomas, and L'Wren Scott.

What do they all have in common? That is correct, suicide! In an instant, each decided, acted and ended their life. See how profound change can be? No more life at all.

It is a harsh example, but that is the point. Change can be harsh, final, drastic, unsettling, and a whole host of other things. In some cases, the result of change is negative, and in others positive.

People that make life-changing decisions in an instant change the course and outcomes of their lives.

Robert John Downey Jr. is an American actor and producer. His career has been characterized by critical and popular success in his youth, followed by a period of substance abuse and legal troubles.

At the age of 5, he made his acting debut in his father Robert Downey Sr.'s film *Pound* in 1970. He subsequently worked with the Brat Pack in the teen films *Weird Science* and *Less Than Zero*. In 1992, Downey portrayed the title character in the biopic *Chaplin*, for which he was nominated for the Academy Award for Best Actor and won a BAFTA Award. Following a stint at the Corcoran Substance Abuse Treatment Facility on drug charges, he joined the TV series *Ally McBeal*, for which he won a Golden Globe Award. He was fired from the show in the wake of drug charges in 2000 and 2001. He stayed in a court-ordered drug treatment program and maintained his sobriety since 2003.

Since Downey decided to stay sober, he went on to star in many movies, including *Tropic Thunder*, for which he was nominated for an Academy Award for Best Supporting Actor. Downey gained global recognition for starring as Tony Stark in ten films within the Marvel Cinematic Universe, beginning with *Iron Man* and leading up to *Avengers: Endgame*. He has also played the title character in Guy Ritchie's *Sherlock Holmes*, which earned him his second Golden Globe.

Downey told Oprah Winfrey in November 2004 that "when someone says, 'I really wonder if maybe I should go to rehab?' Well, uh, you are a wreck, you just lost your job, and your wife left you. Uh, you might want to give it a shot." He added that after his last arrest in April 2001, when he knew he would be facing another stint in prison or another form of incarceration such as court-ordered rehab, "I said, 'Do you know what? I do not think I can continue doing this.' And I reached out for help, and I ran with it. You can reach out for help in kind of a half-assed way, and you will get it, and you will not take advantage of it. It's not that difficult to overcome these seemingly ghastly problems ... what's hard is to decide to do it."

In 2008 Downey starred in two critically and commercially successful films, *Iron Man* and *Tropic Thunder*.

Iron Man was globally released, grossing over $585 million worldwide and receiving rave reviews that cited Downey's performance as a highlight of the film.

Tropic Thunder earned $26 million in its North American opening weekend and retained the number one position for its first three weekends of release. The film grossed $180 million in theaters before its release on home video on November 18, 2008. Downey was nominated for the Academy Award for Best Supporting Actor for his portrayal of Lazarus.

Consider this?!

The first role Downey accepted after *Iron Man* was the title character in Guy Ritchie's *Sherlock Holmes*. Warner Bros. The film set several box office records in the United States for a Christmas Day release, beating the previous record-holder, 2008's *Marley & Me*, by nearly $10M, and finished second to *Avatar* in a record-setting Christmas weekend box office.

Downey returned as Tony Stark in the first of two planned sequels to *Iron Man*, *Iron Man 2*, which was released in May 2010. *Iron Man 2* grossed over $623M worldwide. Downey's other commercial film release of 2010 was the comedy road film, *Due Date*. The movie, co-starring Zach Galifianakis, was released in November 2010 and grossed over $211M worldwide.

In 2012, Downey reprised the role of Tony Stark in *The Avengers*. The film received positive reviews and was phenomenally successful at the box office, becoming the third highest-grossing film of all time both in the United States and worldwide.

Downey played Tony Stark again in *Iron Man 3* (2013), *Avengers: Age of Ultron* (2015), *Captain America: Civil War* (2016), *Spider-Man: Homecoming* (2017), *Avengers: Infinity War* (2018), *Avengers: Endgame* (2019) and three of his scenes from the first Avengers and *Avengers:*

Downey says he has been drug-free since July 2003 and credited his wife with helping him overcome his drug and alcohol habits, along with his family, therapy, meditation, twelve-step recovery programs, yoga, and the practice of Wing Chun kung fu.

When asked why he was able to make his sobriety stick this time on *The Oprah Winfrey Show*, Downey said, "It's really not that difficult to overcome these seemingly ghastly problems. What's hard is to decide to do it."[26]

The rap group N.W.A. comprised of original members Ice Cube (O'Shea Jackson), Dr. Dre (Andre Young), Eazy-E (Eric Wright), DJ Yella (Antoine Carraby), and MC Ren (Lorenzo Jerald Patterson). The group's first album raged against police brutality, racism, and injustice.

Dr. Dre started as the DJ for the World Class Wreckin' Cru in the 1980s. He stepped up to the mic in N.W.A., juggling rhymes and production duties. Aside from NWA, Dre also produced for other Ruthless artists. He later feuded with Eazy-E and Ice Cube. After falling out with the group, Dre left N.W.A. and co-founded Death Row Records with Suge Knight.

Dre left Death Row to form his music empire, Aftermath Entertainment. There, he signed Eminem and helped launch the careers of 50 Cent, The Game, and, more recently, Kendrick Lamar. Dre also co-founded Beats by Dre with Jimmy Iovine. The music streaming service, Beats Music, followed. In 2015, Dre sold Beats Electronics to Apple for a reported $3 billion. Dre banked an estimated 600 million from the sale. The deal instantly positioned Dre as the richest rapper alive.

Ice Cube got his start in a group called C.I.A. He went on to become a founding member of N.W.A. (Cube has a thing for acronyms, it seems). Despite that suspect Jheri curl, Cube was dropping heat. He wrote rhymes for other group members. He penned Eazy-E's "Boyz-N-the-Hood" and contributed to a majority of Eazy-Duz-It.

After leaving NWA, Cube embarked on a remarkable solo run. His first two solo albums, 1990's AmeriKKKa's Most Wanted and 1991's Death Certificate, are considered two of the greatest hip-hop albums of all time. He also teamed up with WC and Mack 10 to form Westside Connection in the mid-90s. The group produced two albums: Bow Down (1996) and Terrorist Threats (2003).

If you discovered Ice Cube in the 2000s, you know him as an actor first. Cube has always had one foot in the studio and one on the movie set. He has starred in major films, including Boyz n the Hood (1991), Barbershop (2002), Are We There Yet? (2005), and 21 Jump Street (2011).

Yella rose with Dr. Dre in the World Class Wreckin' Cru days. He joined NWA and shared production duties with Dre. He also produced records for several Ruthless rappers. Yella went solo in 1996. Shortly after, he retired from music.

Yella had a stint directing adult movies. He has since unretired and is working on a new project.

MC Ren (aka the Ruthless Villain, aka The Villain in Black) was a member of NWA from 1987 until the group's collapse in 1991. After Cube and Arabian Prince left, Ren stepped up and played a bigger writing role in the group. He featured prominently on Eazy-Duz-It, appearing on more than half the songs. Following NWA's messy breakup, Ren stuck with Eazy-E and released mildly successful solo albums on Ruthless.

Post-NWA, Ren took a stab at film production. In 2004, he released an independent, straight-to-DVD movie, Lost in the Game. Ren has since retired from music, although he still drops cameos from time to time.

Arabian Prince is one of the lesser-known members of N.W.A. It is probably because he played a background role and left the group early. Prince, a capable producer, and DJ were there from the start. He left shortly after the group's full-length debut, Straight Outta Compton (1988). Following Ice Cube's return from the Phoenix Institute of Technology in 1988, Prince knew he would be reduced to a bit player. He went on to pursue a solo career, starting with 1989's Brother Arab.

Following his departure, Arabian Prince fought N.W.A. in courts for years to claim his royalties. Today, he performs under the moniker Professor X. He is a mainstay in electro-rap and regularly deejays at local clubs in Los Angeles.

Born and raised in Compton, Eazy-E used the money he saved from selling dope to launch Ruthless Records. In the end, Eazy had beef with Ice Cube and Dr. Dre. The other founding members accused Eazy of misappropriating the group's funds. His solo career was not too shabby—his first solo outing, 1988's Eazy-Duz-It, went double platinum.

After N.W.A.: Eazy had a short-lived solo career before succumbing to AIDs-related complications in 1995. He has been memorialized in rap songs by peers. April 7 is Eazy-E Day in Compton, California.

If you have not seen the movie that documents their journey, I highly recommend it, Straight Outta Compton. The movie demonstrates how even under the worst of circumstances, akin to Oprah's story, in an instant, everything can change and produce extraordinary results.

Sorry, but I am not moving! Something every parent repeatedly hears from their kids at one point or another. It does not sound profound or powerful. It sounds rude and annoying.

However, when Rosa Louise McCauley Parks made that declaration, it rocked society and changed the course of US history. Rosa was born on February 4, 1913, and was an American activist in the civil rights movement best known for her pivotal role in the Montgomery bus boycott. The United States Congress has honored her as "the first lady of civil rights" and "the mother of the freedom movement."

It was on December 1, 1955, in Montgomery, Alabama, Parks rejected bus driver James F. Blake's order to vacate a row of four seats in the "colored" section in favor of a White passenger once the "White" section was filled. Parks was not the first person to resist bus segregation, but the National Association for the Advancement of Colored People (NAACP) believed that she was the best candidate for seeing through a court challenge after her arrest for civil disobedience in violating Alabama segregation laws, and she helped inspire the Black community to boycott the Montgomery buses for over a year. The case became bogged down in the state courts, but the federal

Montgomery bus lawsuit *Browder v. Gayle* resulted in a November 1956 decision that bus segregation is unconstitutional under the Equal Protection Clause of the 14th Amendment to the U.S. Constitution.

Parks' acts of defiance and the Montgomery bus boycott became important symbols of the movement. She became an international icon of resistance to racial segregation and organized and collaborated with civil rights leaders, including Edgar Nixon and Martin Luther King Jr. At the time, Parks was employed as a seamstress at a local department store and was secretary of the Montgomery chapter of the NAACP. She had recently attended the Highlander Folk School, a Tennessee center for training activists for workers' rights and racial equality. Although widely honored in later years, she also suffered for her act; she was fired from her job and received death threats for years afterward. Shortly after the boycott, she moved to Detroit, where she briefly found similar work. From 1965 to 1988, she served as secretary and receptionist to John Conyers, an African-American US Representative. She was also active in the Black Power movement and supported political prisoners in the US.

On June 12, 1987, President Ronald Reagan stood just 100 yards away from the concrete barrier dividing East and West Berlin and uttered some of the most unforgettable words of his presidency: "Mr. Gorbachev, tear down this wall."

By the time Reagan traveled to Berlin, Germany, to commemorate the 750th anniversary of the city's founding, the Berlin Wall had divided the city in half for nearly 26 years. Built and officially closed on August 12, 1961, to prevent disaffected East Germans from fleeing the relative deprivations of life in their country for greater freedom and opportunity in the West, the wall was more than just a physical barrier. It also stood as a vivid symbol of the battle between communism and democracy that divided Berlin, Germany, and the entire European continent during the Cold War.

The wall's origins can be traced back to the years after World War II when the Soviet Union and its Western allies carved Germany into two zones of influence that would become two separate countries, respectively: the German Democratic Republic (East Germany) and the Federal Republic of Germany (West Germany). Located deep within Soviet-controlled East Germany, the capital city of Berlin was also split in two.

Over the next decade or so, 2.5 million East Germans—including many skilled workers, intellectuals, and professionals—used the capital as the primary route to flee the country, especially after the border between East and West Germany was officially sealed in 1952.

Seeking to stop this mass exodus, the East German government closed off passage between the two Berlins during the night of August 12, 1961. What began as a barbed wire fence, policed by armed guards, was soon fortified with concrete and guard towers, completely encircling West Berlin and separating Berliners on both sides from their families, jobs, and the lives they had known before. Over the next 28 years, thousands of people risked their lives to escape East Germany over the Berlin Wall, and some 140 were killed in the attempt.

Despite its later fame, Reagan's speech initially received little media coverage and few accolades at the time. Western pundits viewed it as misguided idealism on Reagan's part, while the Soviet news agency Tass called it "openly provocative" and "war-mongering." And Gorbachev himself told an American audience years later: "[W]e really were not impressed. We knew that Mr. Reagan's original profession was an actor." (Gorbachev added that Reagan had been "courageously cooperative" and a great partner and president.)

According to the former Reagan speechwriter Peter Robinson, who drafted the speech, even Reagan's advisers in the State Department and National Security Council strongly objected, claiming that such a direct challenge would damage the relationship with the

Consider this?!

new Soviet leader Mikhail Gorbachev. The two nations had been moving closer to peace and even disarmament, especially after a productive summit between Reagan and Gorbachev in Reykjavik in October 1986.

Despite this, the Berlin Wall—that heavily fortified symbol of Cold War divisions—seemed as solid as ever.

On June 12, 1987, standing on the West German side of the Berlin Wall, with the iconic Brandenburg Gate at his back, Reagan declared: "General Secretary Gorbachev, if you seek peace, if you seek prosperity for the Soviet Union and Eastern Europe, if you seek liberalization, come here to this gate. Mr. Gorbachev, open this gate." Reagan then waited for the applause to die down before continuing. "Mr. Gorbachev, tear down this wall!"

Reagan's tactics were a departure from his three immediate predecessors, Presidents Richard Nixon, Gerald Ford, and Jimmy Carter, who all focused on a policy of détente with the Soviet Union, playing down Cold War tensions and trying to foster peaceful coexistence between the two nations. Reagan dismissed détente as a "one-way street that the Soviet Union has used to pursue its own aims."

On November 9, 1989, the Cold War officially began to thaw when Egon Krenz, the head of East Germany's Communist Party, announced that citizens could now cross into West Germany freely. That night, thousands of East and West Germans headed to the Berlin Wall to celebrate, armed with hammers, chisels, and other tools. Over the next few weeks, the wall would be dismantled. After talks over the next year, East and West Germany officially reunited on October 3, 1990.

This was a result of changes over two years.

Gorbachev's reforms within the Soviet Union gave Eastern Bloc nations more freedom to determine their government and access to the West. Protests within eastern Germany gained strength, and after

Hungary and Czechoslovakia opened their borders, East Germans began defecting en masse.

I reflected on the words of great people that inspired me. People I respected for their unique perspectives, accomplishments, and profound effect on human culture and history. I was not about to accept the death sentence before my son. Months were simply unacceptable.

During the nine days I spent with my son and the doctors, I spent the remainder of my time researching cancer. I slept for the next few hours. However, I did learn interesting facts about incredible discoveries in the field of cancer.

I also discovered a particular doctor that was seeing remarkable successes with rare cancer protocols he implemented in a country outside the United States. The doctor is well-respected internationally among doctors, yet no one mentioned him to me.

He chose to treat certain people outside the US. The reason is that the United States Food and Drug Administration made it exceedingly difficult to approve these protocols. They simply did not meet certain rigorous clinical trial requirements. As a result, people never saw these treatments and died unnecessarily.

I made the executive decision to take my son to see him. We showed up at his office in Santa Monica, California, and he greeted us after reviewing my son's file and test results. We chatted for a while, and he shared his history and the work he was conducting.

He eventually delivered his professional opinion. He stated that the cancer was an extremely rare cancer with a high mortality rate. The reason, in part, is that it is so rare no one is working on a cure because there is no money in it.

Exactly what no one wants to hear when facing a death sentence!

What proceeded then came as a shock. He explained that while the form of cancer was rare, he believed it exhibited similar characteristics to another type of cancer. A type of cancer that he has seen people survive in his offices overseas. He cautioned that it was only an alternative to consider but not to have hope that it would buy my son years.

I knew in that instant there was more to the story. However, I did not dare ask anything more. The doctor gave me what I was looking for. I looked at my son, and he nodded his head and said let us do it.

Over the next five months, my son underwent chemotherapy treatment. He took the treatment quite well, and it was time for him to be assessed with imaging. I took him to the hospital for scans, and we awaited the results in the radiologist's office.

Eventually, the doctor entered and introduced himself. He was noticeably in a hurry. He blurted out, "okay, let's have a look at the result." He began looking at the images and then cocked his head. "Hold on, I'll be right back," he said.

We assumed he needed the restroom and began chatting. Minutes passed, and he returned. He resumed his review and swiveled around to address us. "In all my years of being a radiologist, I have never seen anything like this." My son and I looked at each other with confusion.

The doctor proceeded, "The cancer is gone! I mean, the cancer is completely gone from your back and appears to be limited to a small tumor and a small portion of bone. It is 85% gone! It is miraculous!"

I was not the least bit surprised. We all exhaled a sigh of relief. "This is great news, and I am giving you everything to take with you to your doctor. I called ahead to his office and got you an appointment, they are waiting for you."

He raced over to the Oncologist, where we received a huge welcome. The Oncologist spoke with us briefly and kept things quite simple. The next step was four months of targeted radiation and three months of chemotherapy thereafter. Within a total of twelve months, my son received the "all clear!"

In an instant, everything can change! And so, it did when we went against the grain and defied the experts. We had been pressured by the most respected doctors in the field to take a completely different course of action. A course that we knew would never get the type of result we achieved. Yes, my son beat the odds of living more than six months.

It only takes an instant to change. The result can be life and not death. Or to the contrary, in the case of Marilyn Monroe, Robin Williams, Sylvia Plath, Kurt Cobain, Kate Spade, Anthony Bourdain, Avicii, Chris Cornell, Hunter S. Thomas, and L'Wren Scott. Had they chosen life, would their contributions have changed anything?

Would the course of human history change? What if Einstein or Hawking took their lives before their great discoveries? Would it change anything? Would their discoveries have surfaced anyway? Yes! The difference, undoubtedly, would be the timing.

Do you agree or not? If you agree, then why? Do you believe in brilliance? I mean, it is not like Einstein, Hawking, or anyone else has superpowers. We see incredible discoveries all the time. Is it because it all is the Block? Perhaps Block Universe is not so farfetched?

Is instant change all it takes to get you closer to where you would like to be? It is up to you! Believe what you wish. See what you wish to see. Do what you wish to do. Does it matter, or does it not? Which side of the bet do you want to be on?

Chapter 13

Why Must We Always Chop Wood, Carry Water?

"There is no substitute for hard work."

—Thomas A. Edison-

Do you want to grow personally or your business? Do you have what it takes to go the distance? Could you benefit from improvement? These are all good and valid good questions to ask yourself. I am not attempting to instill doubt in you or suggest you doubt the ability to succeed.

I am challenging you to improve upon your skills and your chances of success. The best way to get started is by asking yourself questions. Questions that will reveal your Strengths, Weaknesses, Opportunities, and Threats to the most important person of all, you! It is commonly referred to as "doing the work." And, without it, your limitations will impede you, even bring you to a halt.

No journey advances without work. Sometimes we need a reminder to finish a project, a race, or even life. You may not know what exactly is waiting ahead, but the reminder alone can certainly be a wake call and invaluable.

I had that wake-up call years ago. I remember it clear as day. There was a knock at my front door. I answered the door, and a man introduced himself. "Hi, I am Jon, I live across the street, and I want to welcome you to the neighborhood."

"Hi, Jon, nice to meet you. I have my hands full but come on in, have a seat, and I will be right back." He moseyed on in and took a seat. I closed the door and ran upstairs to close the patio doors and then returned.

"So, Keith, what do you do?" he immediately asked.

I found his question an odd opener. Nevertheless, I politely replied, "I'm primarily in real estate," and countered with, "how about you," as I chuckled under my breath.

He replied, "I am in entertainment." "Really, are you, like, a producer or a director?" He looked confused and annoyed, then slowly mumbled, "I guess you could say so."

With a dead straight face, I asked, "have you done anything I might be familiar with?" Again, I had him on the ropes.

"Well, probably. I hope so."

I burst out laughing. "I'm just fucking with you, you're Jon Voight." He smiled and said, "good one, I haven't been suckered like that in quite a long time," and chuckled.

"So, what brings you to the neighborhood?" He continued,

"Well, Jon, I've learned to share more of myself lately, so I'll lay it on the table for you." I went on to tell him my story, which included my recent divorce. How I purchased the how to raise my three kids as a single parent. And all the business projects I was juggling. "Jon, that's my life, and I'm exhausted."

He waited for a moment, and with blue-eyed wisdom, he replied, "Listen, kid, no one said it would be easy and look where you are!" He sat back in the chair and smiled. "Do not worry, kid, you will be fine."

Yes, it has not been easy. However, I am fortunate to have brilliant people pass through my life. Famous people, not famous, and others complete strangers. Regardless of their status, they are people willing to share their wisdom and support. These are moments of Enlightenment and moments you just do not forget.

So why must we always "chop wood, carry water"? If you have never heard the expression, it refers to "doing the work." The origin of the phrase is quite ambiguous. However, most people claim it to be a Zen Proverb. There are also things associated with the phrase.

However, there is no disagreement with the core meaning of the phrase. It means no matter how accomplished we are, how wise or successful, there will always be things we have to do to progress through life. For instance, work to obtain food, clothes, shelter, and more.

Admittedly, when I hear the phrase chop wood carry water, the first thing that comes to mind is chopping down trees. When I was a teenager, I lived in a remote area of New Jersey, and everything was very spread out. To give you an idea, to build a home, you need to have no less than two acres of land. Most properties were enormous, with fruit, vegetable, dairy, and horse farms scattered for miles. We got our food straight from a farm.

When it approached winter, people started to stock up on vital supplies. My friends would go deer hunting to have enough meat during the season. Others chopped down trees like me to have firewood to burn. It was no easy task.

Chopping the tree down was only the beginning. The next step was cutting the tree into logs. We would then stack the logs and cover them so they would dry out and later split the logs into pieces. It was arduous work, especially being out in the cold.

Oftentimes we would be in the snow looking for a dead tree to cut down because we ran out of wood. If we were fortunate enough to find one, they were never close to home. It meant having to transport the wood from the forest back home through the snow. For me, I chopped wood in the physical sense.

Fortunately, we did not have horses like my friends. They did carry the water. During the winter, they would wake up at 5:00 am in the dark, get dressed, and fill buckets with hot water. They would then carry them out to the barns for the horses to drink. As you can imagine, by the time they reached the barns in the freezing cold and sometimes snow, the water was room temperature. Not an easy job.

If you grew up in a city like my kids in Los Angeles and did not have these experiences, it may seem foreign. The phrase might not resonate the same with you. Nevertheless, we all have experiences of having to do strenuous work, whether physical or mental.

So, is the point of chopping wood carrying water merely to have wood and water?

Three-quarters of my childhood friends would agree. However, for most cultures, the meaning is much deeper. The phrase is more generic and more inclusive. And so, it should be.

In fact, it may not even be the best phrase for anything beyond the literal act of chopping wood and carrying water. The phrase implies physical labor. Most people would not find the act of chopping wood and carrying water a pleasant one. In other words, the connotation is a negative one, especially for those who have never done it.

Yes, it's undeniable. We all need to chop wood and carry water, and it is unavoidable. However, should it be unpleasant? I do have memories of chopping wood in the bitter cold and even snow. Memories of carrying unbelievably heavy logs, damaging & fixing chainsaws, breaking & repairing axes, and more. As you can see, there were uncomfortable and frustrating moments that I still have not forgotten.

However, not all the moments were difficult, frustrating, and negative. There were times I was with friends at their homes or mine, working together and conversing while we were chopping wood about things we were experiencing in our lives. Challenges with school, work, sports, family, girls, and so much more. It was an outlet. An opportunity to share and learn from each other and have bonding moments.

I can also tell you about the funniest moments I recall that are even more pronounced than chopping the wood. One time my father realized we were out of wood. We had lost power at our home because of a snowstorm and needed wood for the fireplace because it was freezing in the house. He insisted we go into the woods and find a dead tree to cut down for an immediate supply of wood.

We trekked through the woods and found a dead tree. It was a sizable tree, and he asked me to climb. He wanted me to tie a rope around it so we could tie the rope to another tree and control the direction it fell. We got into a dispute about where to anchor the rope and the direction the tree would fall. Nevertheless, I yielded to him, and he commenced cutting away at the tree.

Before long, the chainsaw had done most of its job. He stopped to take a break, and I tried to broach the subject again about where to tie the tree. I knew it was my last chance to talk before he fired up the noisy chainsaw again. I was concerned the tree would fall in a manner that would make it difficult to transport, but to no avail. I failed to convince him.

He fired up the chainsaw to make the final cuts to land the tree. The tree began to waiver. To my surprise, it was apparent the tree was going in a different direction than either of us expected. I began yelling but could not overcome the buzz of the saw. He realized the tree was coming down and moved out of the way.

It was a sight I will always remember, clear as day. We both stood in amazement as the tree keeled over. I began laughing, and tears filled my eyes. I could see the tree was now headed straight for our house with nothing to stop it.

It was an enormous tree, and neither of us had given any thought to just how big it was. We had trekked a suitable distance into the woods. However, we soon found out just how big the tree was at it impacted the roof of the house. The roof buckled, the rain gutter blew off, and the tree bounced once and then settled into the attic of the house. Ouch!

Recalling the story still makes me laugh. I also remember the valuable things I learned that day about my father, telemetry, and the importance of preparation. It was a wondrous day and a positive experience for me, especially since I did not have to repair the roof.

On the same note, another time, I was cutting logs into smaller pieces with a log splitter. If you are not familiar with a log splitter, it is a type of axe with a long handle and a heavier head that bulges out at the back. The reason is it adds extra weight to the axe to provide more force on the log, making it easier to split the log. Hence a log splitter.

As I was attempting to split a log, I missed the center of the log and hit the handle near the axe head on the edge of the log. The handle split near the axe head, and the handle needed to be replaced. We did not have another handle, so I stopped for the day, straightened out the handle as best I could so the axe head would not fall off the handle, and returned it to the garage.

The following day came, and it was a Saturday. I had gone out with friends the night before and got home early Saturday morning, and it was my day to sleep in. I was a teenager, which meant probably until at least 3:00 in the afternoon.

While I was sleeping away, my father decided to do something he never did. Yes, you guessed it, split logs. He could not find the log splitter because I tucked it away in the garage so no one would see it.

Consider this?!

He came to my room, shook me, and said, where is the log splitter? I need it. Half asleep, I told him it was next to the tool bench in the garage and fell back to sleep.

The next thing I recall was bolting out of my bed in a semi-conscious state. I realized my dad might hurt himself if he was going to use the log splitter. I ran out of the bedroom, down the stairs, and in a panicky voice, asked my mom, where is dad?

She pointed out the kitchen window, and there stood my dad. He was leaning over a giant big tree stump that I used to place logs on top of to split them into pieces. I could see he already had a log on top of the stump and was ready to chop away within seconds. There was no time to warn him!

I told my mom as we watched him swing away. He raised the log splitter from behind his back, over his head, squarely at the log. The head barely caved into the log. The handle snapped, and it caught him off balance. He almost fell over as the handle split from the axe head. It was a scary moment, but we both burst into laughter.

I thought for sure he knew the head was broken and I was in big trouble. My mom looked at me and said, "don't say anything when he comes in. Just let him talk because you're only going to make things worse."

Within two minutes, the door flung open, and in walked my father. I was hiding behind my mother, ready for him to lose his shit. He approached us in the kitchen and stopped squarely in the room. He then said, "You are not going to believe this, I went out to split logs, and I snapped the handle in two." He had the biggest smile on his face, as if he had the strength of Hercules. He thought he broke it because of his strength and not the weakness in the handle.

He grabbed his car keys and said, "I need to go the hardware store to get another handle." After that, he walked off. My mother and I looked at each other and burst into laughter. Typical dad! We did not want to ruin his moment, so we never told him the truth.

My point in sharing the stories is that not all experiences involving chopping wood or carrying water need to be negative. Yes, for my father, the tree incident was negative. However, for me, it was positive. And the log splitter incident for both of us was positive.

We never know what will happen along the way as we chop wood and carry water. We may have negative experiences, or we may have positive experiences. Chopping wood and carrying water is simply something we do along the way.

Therefore, our focus should not be solely on the act. I mean, how valuable are wood and water alone? If you choose to go through life acting without being aware of the bigger picture, you are losing out on a genuine opportunity. It is the knowledge and wisdom you gain from the whole experience related to chopping wood and carrying the water that has the most value.

Yes, we must all chop wood and carry water! However, the next time you find yourself performing what appears to be a mundane task, consider there is something much greater to learn.

Chapter 14

How To Break Barriers?

"There are no constraints on the human mind, no walls around the human spirit, no barrier to our progress except those we ourselves erect."

—Ronald Reagan-

If you want to break barriers, you must first prepare yourself. I do not suppose you would try to break a concrete block with your hand in a single swipe without any practice or preparation. Would you?

Consider viewing breaking barriers like an Olympic athlete preparing for an event. Let us use a hurdler as an example because hurdling is one of the most demanding events in track and field.

You know the athlete than sprints down a track with a handful of competitors leaping over ten evenly dispersed upright wooden barriers. The hurdles are 3.5 feet high for the men and 2.75 feet for the women to clear and are typically made of wattle, which is the wood used to build fences. Hazel or willow is the most common because they make these obstacles incredibly sturdy.

While the hurdles may be of particular importance to the spectators at the event, the hurdles only comprise a fraction of the distance to the finish line. For this reason, hurdlers spend a great deal of time doing more than just practicing jumping over hurdles.

Equally important are strength training, diet, awareness & mental acuity. Hurdlers must strengthen and work on different muscles in their training. Strength training for hurdlers focuses on exercises for the hip flexors, calves, and lower back.

Hurdlers perform what are known as Olympic lifts. Lifts are compound exercises involving multiple muscle groups that include bench presses, squats, deadlifts, and hang cleans. The bench press works the upper body; the squats, legs, and deadlifts work the back and legs, and hang cleans work the hips, knees, shoulders, and elbows. Collectively, they provide the explosiveness one needs when hurdling.

Good nutrition optimizes training programs for hurdlers. A good diet promotes consistency in performance and enhances recovery after workouts and events. Other benefits include maintaining a steady weight and reducing the risk of injury and illness. It also improves confidence and clarity when facing competition.

Basic nutritional guidelines for track & field athletes include eating small meals every two to three hours. Meals to include protein and complex carbohydrates. Staying hydrated with at least eight ounces of water per hour. Eating a post-workout meal within 30 minutes and never skipping meals.

Come race day, they need to be mentally prepared because it is just as important as making sure their body is optimally tuned. They trust their training, control their excitement and try not to get overwhelmed. They stay focused instead of being distracted and visualize success as they take the field.

A great deal of planning, preparation, and work goes into clearing each of the ten hurdles the hurdler must clear before reaching the finish line. The process the hurdlers use is followed by other athletes in other sports as well and is perfect for breaking all sorts of other barriers.

If you want to sprint down the track and glide over the hurdles to the finish line, we can look at how to apply this process to help you clear your barriers.

First, we must recognize the barriers, which are easier said than done. Stimuli are everywhere, bombarding us and making it difficult for us to be laser-focused on our challenges. Therefore, the barriers often seem indistinguishable, vague, or overwhelming.

Second, even if we are fortunate enough to define the barriers, we then must develop a process to overcome them.

Third, we need to be confident we can overcome them.

Fourth, we need to act, which can be frightening because it is perceived as a treacherous journey.

In Chapter 5, we discussed spending a disproportionate amount of time thinking about how to solve problems than solving problems. We also discussed how to solve problems. Here is your next opportunity to put what you learned to work.

Barriers come in all different shapes and sizes. That means so do the solutions to overcoming them. If you view a barrier as a goal, then we know from Chapter 2 and mathematics that they can be achieved. Further, we know from real-world experiences that people constantly do overcome hurdles, both small and large, and not just in the world of sports. Are you feeling more confident?

Before we begin, I want to share a brief story with you. One day I was at home and decided to go outside and retrieve the mail from my mailbox. I rarely checked the mail at home. The reason being all my important mail went to my office. I never gave out my home address because I did not want to get mail in two places.

Accordingly, as you can imagine, the only thing I received at home was junk mail and a substantial amount. In fact, so much that I bought a mailbox two feet high, eighteen inches in width and depth. Therefore, I only needed to check it every four months. Inevitably, there would be something of importance among all the junk.

At any rate, on that day, I felt compelled to check. I walked out the front door and headed to the street where the mailbox sat. When I got to the mailbox, I looked to my right and noticed a guy wearing jeans, a sweatshirt, and a cap. He was standing in my driveway leaning against the wall that sat on the far side of it. He was staring at the ground and shuffling one of his feet as if to amuse himself. He clearly was preoccupied with something.

I thought for a moment, "who is this guy, and why is he in my driveway?" I was living on a private road, so the chances he was lost were next to zero. I thought he must be a friend of someone in the neighborhood and waiting for them. And then it hit me.

It is my neighbor, Mark Wahlberg. Yes, that is him standing in my driveway. He must be back in town to visit his wife and kids. I rarely saw him because he was always away filming movies. So, I decided to say hello.

"Hey, Mark, what's up?"

And, in typical fashion, he replied, "oh hey buddy, I just got back for a few weeks stay," in a quieter than normal voice.

I could tell something was off. "You seem down. Is everything okay?"

He replied, "well, actually, I needed space. I just got back to town from filming, and the kids are running around the house, and my wife wants to move, and it's all a bit much. I hope you do not mind?"

I felt his pain from my own experience. When my wife was pregnant with our third child, we needed to move too. The constant discussion of finding a place was quite intense. Very often, my wife mentioned the topic at less than the optimal time. I knew that unsettling feeling of stress, confusion, and quite possibly even despair.

I chucked and replied, "of course not, you're welcome anytime."

"But I do have a question, if you don't mind?"

"Sure, buddy, what is it?" he said.

"What advice would you give me if I was in your driveway going through the same thing as you?"

Without even hesitating, he looked up at me and said in a strong and confident voice, "Man, I will tell you the most important thing is faith. Without it, you have nothing." And then, with a smile, he continued, "Thanks for reminding me!" And he walked off home.

The point of the story is first, you need to be aware that you have a hurdle or barrier before you and then a strategy to overcome it. Second, once you are aware of the problem, you can turn to your toolbox and grab the skills you need to solve your problem. For Mark, that is his deep belief in faith. And last, once you feel confident, you are armed and ready to act.

Mark was surely aware of his barrier. When I asked him what advice he would give me, it was his opportunity to reach into his toolbox. Once he did, he found his faith or strategy and was ready to head back and implement it to clear the hurdle. It all worked out. He went home, cleared the barrier by agreeing to move, and within weeks began plans to build his new home nearby.

Hopefully, you completed the work in Chapter 9 to better understand your hard and soft skills and feel better about your abilities. Also, if you completed the affirmations and you are implementing them and stating them daily, then you should be experiencing more positivity and confidence daily.

I am confident you now possess the mindset to overcome your barriers, and you should, too. First, you are aware your single greatest challenge is yourself. Second, I shared information with you on how to identify, evaluate, and improve your hard and soft skills. Third, information that you might not have found on potentiality is on your radar.

Yes, controversial topics were thrown at you. You may believe all or none are true. Whatever your choice, it is fine. The important thing is you are open to innovative ideas that can change your perspective, your actions, and your life.

It is time to start breaking your barriers. Recall Chapter 9, where we discussed hard and soft skills. We also discussed how to identify and evaluate them through a SWOT analysis. If you found the technique helpful and you were happy with the results, then you may apply the same process here.

Once again, it is time to get relaxed and comfortable before identifying your barriers. Do your breathing exercise, take a walk, or meditate. The choice is yours!

Next, write down a single goal you are looking to achieve. Do not confuse yourself by thinking you need to achieve more than one goal to realize a single goal. As I mentioned earlier, conciseness and simplicity are important. Taking one thing at a time is critical.

Also, vague goals will undoubtedly complicate your efforts. You will experience delays and quite possibly incubate frustration and stress. The frustration and stress will wear away at your positivity, undermine your confidence, and challenge your work. Keep it simple and make it easier on yourself.

Identify the single goal you want to achieve. Next, quickly list the barriers you sense are related to achieving the specific goal. One or two-word descriptions are best. Do not overthink them. And finally, take your hour break to let the dust settle.

Welcome back! It's time to execute the drill one more time. Review your work, and add or subtract any barrier you feel belongs or does not. Next, write down an explanation for each barrier. The explanation should include: Why is it a barrier? Why do you perceive it to be a barrier, and how do you envision overcoming the barrier? If you can produce more questions to answer even better.

Allow your list to ruminate. You can return to it later to see if you are in alignment with your last round of thoughts. If you have not figured it out, one of the objectives we are addressing through the process is confidence.

The more work you do before you commence your action, the more confidence you will have when it comes time to execute your plan. What we are talking about is no different from doing your homework in school in preparation for an exam. The difference here is we are not in school practicing for the real world. Instead, it is the real world. It is exam time now!

It is Go Time! Time to evaluate the solutions you envisioned to clear the barriers you perceive. Are the solutions realistic? What steps are needed to overcome each hurdle? Similarly, hurdle races sometimes include hurdles of different heights.

Therefore, it is essential to be concise and comprehensive with your solutions. There should be multiple steps for each solution. There may even be ambiguities with your solution. In these situations, you will need, at the minimum, a plan B and C. Remember, you do not want to lose time if you need to pivot.

For more complex problems, consider engaging more people. It may be another person or a group. Why? Because two heads can be better than one when it comes to solving complex problems.

In Chapter 5, we covered the process and benefits of adding more people to the mix. As much as it may feel awkward to engage others, consider the consequences of excluding them. It may cost you significantly more time to solve the problem. Even worse, what if you fail to arrive at a solution? The choice is yours.

In conclusion, you will inevitably encounter barriers on the way to realizing your goals. Being realistic, that it requires work and a great deal is a good start. You may even need the help of others. And that is perfectly fine.

You already have the knowledge to overcome significant barriers. As you face new challenges and conquer them, you will gain invaluable experience and added confidence to take on even bigger challenges.

We discussed the process of a hurdler and all the preparation that goes into training for a race, what they must do, how they prepare, and what happens when it is time to perform.

I will leave you with a brief story that parallels and reinforces what is necessary to perform your best.

It was the summer of 1980. I spent the day with my photographer friend, Bill Mark. A well-known photographer of the time photographed famous athletes and celebrities. Bill knew everyone. He was quite a colorful and charismatic character. Everyone loved him and being a subject.

We were at the US Open at Baltusrol in Springfield, New Jersey. A course I knew quite well. I grew up nearby and always enjoyed visiting, especially when there was a tournament.

It was a long, sweltering day, and there were unexpected performances. There were newcomers with great performances and veterans with less-than-expected performances. It was quite exciting and disappointing as the players vied for the top positions.

Toward the end of the tournament, we took positions near the greens. Bill insisted because we were nearing the end, and it was time to get more shots on the greens. The greatest players passed through, but one in specific made an impression I will never forget.

Arnold Palmer made it to the green. His ball was sitting far from the pin. The terrain was very uneven, with an awkward curvature to the cup. It was at least two shots away.

Arnold took his time looking at the green. He squatted down to get a view of the path to the pin. He then got up, backed away, and walked to another spot to squat and get another look. He proceeded to do this repeatedly to get different views or perspectives.

As a spectator, I was hot and getting impatient. We all knew he was going to make it in two shots. He finally approached the ball and took a couple of practice swings. Finally, he is ready to putt. He then backed away to get one last glimpse from another spot.

He returns to the ball. Takes more practice swings and then stops. Now it was time. He adjusted his footing, looked at the pin, and then gave the ball a nice tap.

Lo-and-behold, as we wait and watch, with bated breath, the ball careens across the green and dribbles into the cup. It was nothing less than spectacular.

Bill rushed the green yelling, "Arnold, Arnold, how about a few photos?" "Absolutely Bill, for you I'd give you my balls!" as he laughed. When Bill was finished taking his photos, I said to Arnold, "that was an amazing putt! What is your secret?" He leaned over, put his hand on my shoulder, looked straight into my eyes, and replied, "Do not let anyone distract you. Concentration is everything!"

As you continue to improve yourself, stay relaxed and consistent, regularly do the work, and enjoy the process. Challenges may seem insurmountable. However, just as Arnold made a near-impossible shot. So can you! You have the tools, and with practice, you will rise. "Do not let anyone distract you. Concentration is everything!"

Chapter 15

What Does It All Mean?

"It is ok to be confused. Confusion is the route to all clarity in the world."

—Shah Rukh Khan-

We are constantly inundated with information. The bulk of that information is irrelevant. In other words, we glean extraordinarily little information of value.

As an entrepreneur, we see even more information in our quest to master our skills and conquer our goals. We are searching for specific information to develop something that is unique. And it is not an effortless process.

With a vast sea of information, how can you not be confused at times? It is perfectly normal. To be a successful entrepreneur, it is imperative to develop your skills to sift through information quickly.

I am aware I have presented a significant amount of information in this book. I have also shared theories and scientific principles that may be foreign to you. It would not surprise me at all if you were confused about the information presented.

Therefore, I feel it is important to use this chapter to recap what we have covered. Because the book is meant to help you achieve success. Therefore, I want to clarify and tie everything together in a meaningful way to succeed.

In Chapter 1, you were given the opportunity to revisit your childhood. It is not so easy for everyone to do. I hope it reactivated your memory and brought back fun and interesting memories. It certainly did for me.

It is also a considerable time in our lives because it is our formative years. A time when we are very malleable and open to suggestions. Influence is never more profound, and our desire to learn and believe is even stronger.

Have you previously considered the veracity of the things you learned when you were younger? It is remarkable how much we learn that proves to be false. It is also remarkable that we are all impacted either directly or indirectly by falsehoods, whether we are aware of it or not.

On the other side, if you are brave enough to acknowledge that much of what you learn in your formative years is false, it can be extremely helpful. You may ask how it may be helpful. It is water under the bridge.

However, it is an opportunity to see life from a new perspective. That perspective is the truth. We are talking night and day. It may alter your path, open doors of opportunity, and even your chances of success.

Are you willing to be flexible about the veracity of the information you receive as you move forward in your life? In other words, be open to more possibilities. It is a characteristic or trait of all great entrepreneurs. Do you possess it?

In Chapter 2, we discussed this moment that you lack the awareness of knowledge or experience to reach your goal now. It seems like an obvious statement. If you did have the awareness and knowledge at this moment, you wouldn't be chasing the goal.

I provided you with an opportunity to consider analyzing statements. Additionally, I shared a practice to help you prepare for your analysis. And I shared an example of using basic math to reduce or eliminate uncertainty.

The point of sharing the process of solving problems with math goes beyond reducing or eliminating uncertainty. Suppose you were facing a series of challenges. Can you guess what other benefit there may be?

It may come to you if you think about the TV Show Jeopardy or America Ninja Warrior. Jeopardy challenges mental skills, and conversely, American Ninja Warrior challenges physical skills. However, they have one thing in common. Want to guess?

Contestants start with simple questions or obstacle challenges. As contestants overcome the question or obstacle, they are then faced with a more challenging question or obstacle to complete. As the contestants answer more questions and complete more obstacles, you can see them gain confidence. It is often reflected by them risking more money or displaying more comfort as they attempt to tackle the next obstacle.

Reducing and eliminating uncertainty is a powerful tool. It can often be done with basic math, as I demonstrated. By reducing or eliminating risk, you may boost your confidence to help you tackle even more intimidating challenges.

In Chapter 3, we discussed you do not create anything. It is a controversial chapter in the book. I shared with you the definition of creativity and imagination. We also discussed the Block Universe.

It is funny to me that you can imagine something and bring it into creation. It is perfectly acceptable according to the dictionary and science. However, if you can imagine something but fail to bring it into existence, then you need to wait for the dictionary and science to adopt it.

Fortunately, In the case of the dictionary, we need not wait as long. I remember when I was a kid, the word "ain't" was unacceptable because it did not appear in the dictionary. However, after a handful of years and ridicule sessions, it was finally admitted to the dictionary.

Remarkably, someone dared to invent something called Urban Dictionary in 1999. It was not invented with the purpose to help less educated get their vernacular recognized. Rather, it was invented to help cultures understand each other and communicate better.

Again, another falsehood is that should you live in an urban area, you are less educated. It is embarrassing! Tell me, who are the dictionaries and scientific journals serving? Aristocrats?

Brilliant people live everywhere! I do not think anyone can argue about the fact after the COVID pandemic. Do we really need these types of limitations in our lives? How long do we need to wait to believe in something like Block Universe?

In Chapter 4, we discussed if we only keep 20%, or less, of what we learn, then why spend time trying to remember as much as we can? I discussed the things we are asked to memorize that are pointless.

Information was presented on how the brain functions. I compared the human brain to a typical personal computer. Both have memory systems such as working memory, short-term, and long-term memory in the case of the human brain. Similarly, a computer has RAM or Random Access Memory and a Hard Drive. By comparison, the human brain has 625 times more storage space. However, in both cases, neither has infinite memory.

Hopefully, after reading Chapter 8, you have a new perspective on stockpiling information. Should we be more mindful of the valuable time we spend attempting to memorize things? How about what we chose to memorize?

In Chapter 5, we discussed you spend a disproportionate amount of time thinking about how to solve problems than solving problems. I shared the comments of brilliant minds, such as Henry Ford and Albert Einstein. Their respective views on problem-solving time and perspective.

You got a glimpse into the latest problem-solving research affecting Corporate America. The data is undeniable. Companies are dealing with employee performance to optimize their businesses and profits. They know the truth, and so should you!

I shared methodologies to help you solve problems yourself or in a group setting. One method is a basic approach that I recommend you learn at the minimum. The other methodology is for more complex problems and employs others to gain multiple perspectives. It may also produce multiple solutions.

We also got to see the invaluable SWOT analysis. How to use it to identify Strengths, Weaknesses, Opportunities, and Threats. It is one of my personal favorites. I highly recommend it.

Last, I gave you a specific example of the importance of having a problem-solving process at the ready. It could be the difference between life and death!

In Chapter 6, we discussed you are not in flow! I gave you an example of how people often mistake being in the state of flow. It is primarily because they are unaware of the various states that must all be present.

I shared what people often mistake as flow. I call it auto-pilot, but it is more commonly referred to as classical conditioning. Operating under the wrong assumption can be frustrating, at the least. It can cause you to discard a scientifically recognized state. It is one that provides a tremendous advantage, and you do not want to miss it.

In Chapter 7, we discussed everyone has the same single biggest challenge. Knowing everyone has the same single biggest challenge is invaluable information.

First, once you are aware of the single biggest challenge, you now know where you need to focus. If you have your eyes scattered and you are looking in multiple places for answers, you will waste time and distribute your efforts. Doing so will produce less than optimal results.

Second, by knowing the truth, you will eliminate unnecessary barriers. Without those obstacles, your confidence will soar. Your chance of success will also dramatically improve.

You will need to chop wood and carry water. However, you will see a drastic improvement in your skills, and the results will show in your life.

Last is something I did not mention in the chapter. It relates to others. Sometimes, you find another person or others struggling with a matter. As you observe them battling to overcome the challenge, you will better understand the behavior they exhibit. They may even project that behavior onto you. Know their challenge is an internal one. You may not take things personally and be more sympathetic and help them through a challenging time.

In Chapter 8, we discussed you have access to more knowledge than you need. I shared data to give you a better perspective on how much information we have access to and are yet to discover. I also shared scientific discoveries.

The scientific discoveries include proven science and theories yet to be proven. The validated science includes thoughts, information, data, and energy. The scientific theories include Block Universe and Quantum Field Theory. I also shared the New Thought spiritual belief known as the Law of Attraction because it, too, is being examined scientifically, just not by mainstream scientists.

Within the past one hundred years, science has validated considerable theories because of advances in technology. The advances in technology are continuing to grow exponentially. There are undoubtedly more discoveries and validation on the horizon.

In the meantime, it is up to you to take advantage of what is scientifically proven and yet to be validated. These are valuable tools you should not ignore in your quest for success. I encourage you to keep an open mind and continue to chop wood and carry water.

In Chapter 9, we looked at skills being like tools. They work best when sharpened. Skills are the tools in your toolbox to help you achieve success. It is imperative to take inventory of those tools and examine them. Are they in need of sharpening or repair, or should they be discarded?

It is also essential to know the differences between the skills. Hard skills are your academic and technical skills. Soft skills are your people or skills. Employers look closely at both to determine if you are worthy of an interview.

In an entrepreneurial setting, you were given the opportunity to categorize your skills and assess them using a SWOT analysis. You should now have a much better understanding of skills and abilities.

Last, we touched on affirmations. Affirmations are positive statements that are utilized to reinforce positive beliefs and bolster confidence. You will find a noticeable improvement in your state of being, performance, and results with more positivity and confidence.

In Chapter 10, we discussed life is more enjoyable having positive experiences. Here you were given the science behind the five substances that affect your happiness. They are dopamine, endorphin, serotonin, oxytocin, and cortisol.

The science is well-established and unambiguous. There are things you can do that require little effort to improve the balance of each. I highly recommend mastering them as you would your diet or exercise routine.

Feeling happier will lead to better clarity and performance. You will also have more positive experiences. Therefore, understanding and optimizing these substances is critical if you want to realize the benefits.

You will notice a tremendous difference in your mental states and efforts within a brief period after you begin your new happiness regime. Paying attention to the cues that are produced is an opportunity to re-evaluate and rebalance. With greater awareness, happiness, and a healthier lifestyle, you can dramatically improve your mood, experiences, focus, productivity, and chances of success.

In Chapter 11, we discussed the primary benefit of working with others is not achieving a common goal. When you are an entrepreneur, you are among a select few that choose to realize a dream that others would find impossible or not worth the journey.

The mindset of the janitor at NASA helping to put a man on the moon is genius. And in all fairness, everyone has those moments of genius. However, it takes more than just an idea. It takes planning, execution, insight, diligence, perseverance, and more.

You are the entrepreneur with the ideas and skills to execute and deliver. The goal is yours. You are running the show, and it is up to you to deliver results. Yet, you need others to help. So, you recruit others, like the janitor, to come along for the ride.

Your dream becomes his dream, and along the way, you are mastering your soft skills. You stay up on the latest trends and competitors to stay even or maintain your lead while improving and adding to your hard skills.

As you improve upon each of your hard and soft skills, you are making progress. Your team is also sharpening its skills. Yet, you are aware there is more to it. It is the culmination of your thoughts and everyone's improvement in their skills that eventually produce the results that spill over.

You, your colleagues, as well the other participants reap the rewards. The payoff is exhilarating without exception, and everyone is ecstatic and amazed. And why? Because you and your associates achieved something greater than yourself.

In Chapter 12, we discussed an instant of change could transform a life forever. Do you know the top five regrets of the dying:

1. I wish I'd had the courage to live a life true to myself, not the life others expected of me.
2. I wish I hadn't worked so hard.
3. I wish I'd had the courage to express my feelings.
4. I wish I had stayed in touch with my friends.
5. I wish that I had let myself be happier.25

What is success to you? How serious are you about achieving it? Do you plan to do it in this lifetime? Or will you be addressing these questions when it comes time for you to check out?

Success is about choices! Achieving it will not be easy. It involves risk and failure. Unless you are Jim Morrison, Kate Spade, Kurt Cobain, Marilyn Monroe, or the like, you can always retreat or pivot.

Yes, making decisions can be intimidating and scary. I have shared stories to demonstrate exactly how intimidating and scary they can be. It does not take balls to decide; it is the contrary. Failing to act or putting your fate in someone else's hands is what should scare you.

At this moment, you have the skills to succeed and achieve wonderful things in your life. Do not doubt yourself! Yes, you will need to work to improve those skills. However, you will build confidence along the way and get comfortable with tough decisions and change. I know it to be true because I have that experience. Remember, without change, there is no transformation!

In Chapter 13, we discussed why we must always chop wood and carry water. "Listen, kid, no one said it would be easy," the words of Jon Voight. Over the years, Jon and I have agreed and strongly disagreed on issues. When he spoke those words, they resonated with me. However, our interpretation differed.

Jon is the same vintage as my father. Their generation famously chose to perceive life as "a battle." Hence, "no one said it would be easy." However, my generation, the baby boomers, chose to perceive it as "a challenge." And fortunately, Millennials and Gen-Z see it as a journey, and simply, "it is what it is."

I recommend you give serious consideration to how you plan to perceive your path to success. Are you looking to be occupied with surviving a battle? Are you looking to focus on conquering a challenge? Or do you prefer being present to acquire all the knowledge you can while you enjoy the journey? Before you start chopping and carrying.... choose wisely!

In Chapter 14, we discussed how to break barriers. I used the sport of hurdling as an example because it is considered the most demanding of all sports in terms of preparation and training. Physical condition alone is not sufficient to win a race.

The important critical elements of top performance include awareness, physical training, and mental acuity. It is important to know the difference between awareness and mental acuity.

Awareness is the knowledge or perception of a situation or fact. Mental acuity is a measure of the brain's ability to respond to stimuli. It accounts for the speed and quality of the response.

I used the example involving my neighbor Mark to illustrate how we can be aware of a situation and the barrier before us. However, due to stress or other things, we may lack the awareness to open our tools box, grab the skill or skills we need, fix the problem, or clear the barrier.

When you forget to chop wood or hone your skills, your mental acuity begins to decline. Breaking barriers gets more challenging. In other words, you must maintain your skills at the minimum, and that requires practice. Remaining alert during the process and your skills will improve. Do you know what you need to claim success? Start breaking those barriers!

Chapter 16

Where To Start?

"Even the greatest was once a beginner. Don't be afraid to take the first step."

—Muhammad Ali-

Everyone loves a day off, especially a kid in school. That was me one day back in 1977. My dad woke me in the morning and told me he had a surprise. My dad was always tight-lipped, so asking was pointless. I got ready for school and walked downstairs to have some breakfast. Not a word from him as we ate. "Alright, it is time to head off," he said.

We got in the car and headed down the long driveway. At the bottom, he paused the car. He looked over at me and said, "I think you will remember today for many years to come." What exactly does that mean, I thought to myself.

He then proceeded and made a right out of the driveway. I knew we were not going to school. I was excited! Turning right meant we were off for an adventure. Another day off from school. And usually, going to New York City, but for what?

We continued to route 22, and that confirmed my suspicion. I fell asleep and soon opened my eyes to the cobblestone street and the old brownstones that lined the street. Yes, it's New York, as we bumped along the road.

"So, where are we going?" I asked. Nothing, absolutely nothing, as we continued onto the FDR Drive heading uptown. I closed my eyes again and soon awoke to Madison Avenue. "You are going to love this," he said.

He parked the car and touted, "hop out of the car and meet me in the limo behind us." I looked several cars back and could see a jet-black Lincoln limousine sitting idle. Why would we be taking a limousine somewhere if we already have a car?

Nevertheless, I rolled out of the car and approached the limo. I could not see anyone in the car, no driver, just black windows. It appeared to be empty. I opened the door, leaned forward, and tucked my head in. The next words were iconic. "Good Morning, Champ!"

I glanced over to the words and became weak. Should I fall, get in the car, or have someone wake me up? There he sat, responsible for the first bet I ever lost in my life to my third-grade teacher, Ms. Lindsay. I am clearly dreaming!

Silence, I was speechless, feeling stupid, proud, and excited. "Hi, nice to meet you!" I stuttered. "Get in the car and shut the door while we wait for everyone," he spoke.

It is as if it were yesterday. My idol sitting before me — what every kid dreams about. It was intimidating, scary, and pure adrenaline. He was big, powerful, charismatic, larger than life, and that was on TV. It all paled in caparison with him now sitting in front of me, the Champ, Muhammad Ali!

I had the honor and privilege to spend time alone and chat with the Champ as we waited. He asked me questions one after another and joked at every chance he got. It was fun, awkward, and exciting. I got to spend the whole day with him, my dad, and his friends. I learned a great deal from him on that day.

I soon got to spend a few hours again with him again on October 1, 1977, at Pele's farewell game at Giants Stadium before a sold-out crowd and a global television audience estimated at 500 million. Another remarkable day, spending time with the Champ and briefly meeting Pele and his wife.

Over the decades that followed, I would see Muhammad periodically. Words never were sufficient to describe him, then or even now. The last time I saw him was in 2004 at the Beverly Wilshire Hotel in Beverly Hills. I was on the elevator and stopped on one of the floors on my way down. The doors opened, and there he was in a light brown suit. He smiled at me, reached for his sleeve, and whipped out a bouquet of flowers.

I never expected to see him, and certainly, him performing magic. He handed the flowers to me, winked, and whispered, "Keith, you know I need those back?" It was a great laugh, the last I would see of him, our last magical moment.

However, for me, the most memorable moment was on the first day we met. It was in the limo. He said to me, "always remember, if you can see it, and your heart believes it, you can achieve it," with a quick shuffle of punches. The Champ was not only inspirational but empowering. I am forever grateful for the moments and wisdom he shared.

Muhammad shared other words of wisdom, "Even the greatest was once a beginner. Don't be afraid to take the first step." It is now time for you to prepare for that step!

Muhammad never got in the ring without getting prepared. Every fight required extensive training. It was months and months of training. It is the same for all great athletes, performers, executives, and successful people. You should expect the same of yourself before taking the next big step in an endeavor.

You start by taking a good hard look at yourself. If you completed the SWOT Analysis on your hard and soft skills, as I recommended earlier in the book, then you are positioned well. Because your hard work will soon be put to the test, and you will need objectivity and honesty to achieve success.

The second step is addressing your motivation. We talked about internal and external motivation earlier. You need to be absolutely clear on the matter. Your determination to succeed will undoubtedly be challenged at some point. I am talking about an extreme test. Do you want to wait to be pushed to the breaking? In other words, do you want to spend time and effort and then find out you are not willing to go the distance to succeed?

Once you are clear on your motivation, you should feel confident that between your motivation and skills, you will succeed. I cannot overemphasize the point. The combination of internal motivation and mastering skills is the core of your success. Yes, you will need to chop wood and carry water to develop your skills like Michael Jordan, 90,000 missed shots.

However, improving your skills as you execute your plan with determination is where it is. Everyone has internal motivation and skills. You have what you need. The question is whether you will make the most of it to increase your chances of success.

Third, are you willing to change? The kind of change that produces a vastly different result than you are accustomed to. Are you willing to change for a different future at a cost? Are you willing to accept substantial disruption in your daily life as you know it? These are important questions to answer.

Consider this?!

Most people answer no, and it is by no coincidence. The reason, our brain is hardwired to resist change, and for a good reason. It is a protection mechanism.

The portion of the brain I am referring to is called the amygdala. It is one of two almond-shaped clusters located deep within the middle of the brain's cerebrum. The primary role is in the processing of memory, decision-making, and emotional responses that include fear, anxiety, and aggression. And it keeps us from doing stupid or harmful things that could cost our lives.

In other words, it is not going to be as simple as saying I will change, and everything falls in place. We are dealing with a counterintuitive function that presents a continuous challenge. The challenge is overcoming the amygdala's agenda and dealing with the hormones it releases that are associated with fear, fight, or flight.

Mastering the amygdala will take work. The thought may seem unpleasant. However, consider it an opportunity to address your feelings. Because that is exactly what you will be doing as the chemicals it releases trigger your emotions.

More important than the work. The process will require a level of awareness sufficient to keep matters in the proper context. Once you are aware the amygdala is back on the job playing with your emotions, you will be able to make conscious choices that are in your best interest, transcend the hormones and emotions, and affect the change you desire.

Even organizations, when presented with a new initiative, which is not only good with tons of benefits, will resist it. However, there is good news.

We can overcome the psychological costs of change that stand in the way of our happiness and success by focusing on three things.

1. Dissatisfaction with our present situation or circumstances.
2. Maintaining a positive vision of our future.

3. Developing the steps to make our vision a reality.

There is a formula that addresses these factors for success. The formula was created by David Gleicher in the 1960s and provides a model to assess the relative strengths affecting the likely success of organizational change programs.

Gleicher's Formula is as follows:

$D \times V \times F > R$

Dissatisfaction x Vision x First Steps > Resistance

In other words, the pain of loss is greater than the power of gain.

Isn't this wonderful? We now have a better understanding of the bigger picture and where to start. Yes, I am unhappy with my situation. Yes, I am willing to change. Yes, I understand it is not effortless because my mind has its agenda. I will need to deal with my brain and my emotions. However, I am aware of the situation, what needs to be done, and the fact that I possess what is needed to overcome the challenges.

Next, are there any other challenges that need to be identified? What are they, and how may I overcome them?

You are identifying challenges, understanding them, and what you need to overcome them. Can you see how you are breaking it down into manageable steps? Do you see how to develop a systematic approach to overcoming each challenge? Can you see how doing your homework first will allow you to get off on the best footing? Do you now feel more confident you can achieve what you desire? Good, because confidence is essential to achieving your goal. Without it, you will surely quit.

I am proud of you for identifying your tools, challenges, and doing your homework. I know your chances of succeeding are dramatically greater than others, and so should you. You are now ready for the last step.

Consider this?!

Finally, you need to develop your plan. You have everything else to succeed, the tools, motivation, and mindset. Developing your plan will be much easier than you think.

It is similar to putting a model car or airplane together. You have all the parts and tools (hopefully sharpened), and you know what it will look like when it is complete. What you do not have are the instructions and the plan.

Again, you are only solving one unknown variable, but it is the easiest. Why? Because you have all the parts and can figure out how they fit together, at the absolute worst case, by using trial and error. In other words, you will succeed. It is just a question of how long it will take.

No one likes trial and error. I don't suggest you begin with trial and error. I do suggest you lay out all the parts. In other words, determine the parts needed and organize them before you start putting them together.

Once you have organized them or put them in order, take a break. Leaving your work and clearing your mind is a practice you have done and know by heart. You may return with a clear mind, re-evaluate your work, and restructure as needed to optimize the plan.

You have invested a tremendous amount of your time and effort. Is there any reason you are not confident you will succeed? If not, address your concern and get it resolved. When you are confident in your plan and yourself, you are then ready to start executing your plan. Remember, you do not need luck. You have something much greater, like Stefan Mandel, who won the lottery. You have certainty!

Chapter 17

How To Reach The Finish Line!

"Keep your eyes on the finish line and not on the turmoil around you."

—Rihanna-

Congratulations, you are approaching the finish line! I know you are smart. Much of what we have discussed throughout the book, you already know. However, will you be smart enough to implement the other things you learned? Will you revisit the processes and techniques we discussed to understand, solidify, reaffirm, and strengthen your beliefs to impact your future?

Is it really necessary? Consider the scuba diving story I shared with you. The diver was well-trained. He also possessed many years of experience. Yet, when put in peril, his lack of process nearly cost him his life. Will you be ready when you are put in a challenging situation? Or will you be ready to capitalize when timing meets opportunity?

If you do not continually ask these types of questions, your chances of succeeding diminish. You must be ready. Unquestionably, you are going to meet challenges along the way. Challenges that aim at your tools and confidence. They will far exceed anything you have yet to experience. Ask any successful entrepreneur, and they will tell you it is true.

I do not want you to fail. It will be a long journey, and the stakes will be high. The distractions will be intermittent at the least or even constant. "Don't let anyone distract you. Concentration is everything!" Said Arnold Palmer.

I am your coach, and I am telling you to get ready. I trust you did the work.

Before you head out to perform your best, I want to share some things with you.

First, step back and learn to be present. Being present means being fully conscious of the moment and free from distraction. Earlier in the book, I shared how the brain processes information.

We are constantly being bombarded with stimuli. The stimuli that happen to get captured are sent to the brain through neurons. The brain interprets the stimuli, processes the information, and then reacts.

When you are not present, you capture fewer stimuli or even false stimuli. Therefore, the brain receives less stimuli and has fewer information to interpret and issue a response. Accordingly, the response is less than optimal.

As an example, I was recently in Tulum on a cloudy evening with a friend, and we noticed many baby turtles heading into the courtyard of the hotel. We had no idea what was happening.

We went to the office of the hotel and shared the news because we were concerned about the turtles. We found a woman and explained the situation, and she was just as confused. So, we asked her to follow us to the courtyard.

When we returned to the courtyard, we found the groundskeeper corralling the turtles. The woman asked the veteran groundskeeper what was going on, and he explained that they were being attracted by the light in the courtyard because it was the only visible light. He planned to corral them and return them to the ocean.

It turns out that when sea turtles are born, they are attracted to light. Therefore, they crawl to the brightest light. When they are on a dark beach, it is simple. They crawl toward the moonlight that guides them to the ocean.

However, in this case, it was a cloudy night, and the only light was in the courtyard of the hotel. Accordingly, they headed in the opposite direction. They were under the false impression they were headed to the ocean.

In other words, the stimulus was the light. The courtyard light, not the moonlight. The false reading caused the turtles to choose the wrong direction. A direction that could have led to a hazardous outcome.

The same thing could happen to you if you are not present. I do not want to see you headed in the wrong direction unnecessarily. Fortunately, you can evaluate a situation and make a correction. Nevertheless, mistakes can cost you time, money, and more.

Other benefits you will receive by remaining present are improved attention, vitality, confidence, and happiness. I highly recommend it.

Second, accept you will need to chop wood and carry water. I shared with your stories of many celebrities that had to deal with challenges that required incredible work.

It is not only celebrities that face these challenges. Einstein and Steven Hawking had their challenges. Einstein suffered physically and mentally from stress. He got divorced, lost his children, and had to put his work on halt because of World War II because he was Jewish. Steven Hawking was diagnosed with ALS at 21, and his health decline confined him to a wheelchair and a difficulty to communicate verbally.

Elon Musk faced failure when PayPal was voted the worst business idea of the year in 1999. In 2008, Tesla stood on the brink of collapse due to insufficient finances. He decided to go bankrupt and used the money he earned from the sale of PayPal to continue. Two years later, Elon was officially tapped out. Fortunately, loans from friends help him survive. Musk nearly imploded with SpaceX with three failed rocket launches. He scraped together parts and the last of his resources for a final fourth launch and succeeded. It catapulted SpaceX into a highly profitable company.

Do not expect your challenges to be any less. You will need to chop wood and carry water. When you are an entrepreneur, everything is relative. You will experience extreme stress and need to continue to chop wood and carry water.

Your ability to successfully navigate through those stressful times will determine your success. You need not solve the theory of relativity or put a man on Mars to succeed, but do not think your stress level will be any less as you work than people who achieved much greater success. However, keep in mind what my friend Ian Copeland would say, "Stress in life should be like a Bacardi & Coke, light on the calories."

Third, learn to be an observer instead of making judgments. First, you need to understand we all have automatic thoughts. Second, you need to be aware of your thought process. Mastering the technique will allow you to intervene before you make a bad decision.

Meditation is an excellent example. You sit down, close your eyes, and let your brain populate your mind with thoughts if it has not already. Watch the thoughts but do not get emotional about anything. Pretend you are watching a movie. When you are done watching, then take some notes on what you saw and leave them. You then return at a later time with a fresh mind and review them.

I enjoy the process of correspondence I receive. I noticed many years ago that lawyers always send important things on Friday at 5:00

pm. If I would read the correspondence, it would oftentimes ruin my weekend. Therefore, I have a practice of not reviewing anything from lawyers until Monday. I then read it, take notes on anything important, and then let it sit. Last, I return hours or days later and review it when I am relaxed and calm.

Remember the following:
1. You are not your thoughts. Do not believe everything you think.
2. Our brain is wired for survival. At times, it has its agenda, and we need to intervene.
3. Our brain produces automatic thoughts. Do not get emotional; just observe them objectively.
4. Do not get swept away in unnecessary drama when times get challenging. You have the choice to stay calm and act intelligently and rationally.

Being the observer is a wonderful tool to have in your toolbox. It will serve you well. It will keep your stress to a minimum and lead to better decisions.

Fourth, accept that change is necessary. You are an entrepreneur, a leader, not a follower. You seek impact! And that requires thinking creatively and change. You need to accept it and be ready.

Your mindset is paramount to achieving success. Therefore, you want to position yourself for success. The best way to do that is to view change as an opportunity to gain experience and realize the success you seek. Get excited about what is waiting for you, and look forward to each moment as a fun adventure.

Get ready! Start implementing change in your life to get comfortable. Take small steps. Get out of the opposite side of the bed in the morning. Drink at least a tall glass of water with every meal. As you implement changes that serve you better, you will see the results.

Place a value on the things you do. Have a reason to do them. Make chopping the wood and carrying the water worth the effort. Acknowledge the benefits and be present as you enjoy the rewards. Give more thought to the benefits, opportunities, and possibilities. Consider the value of personal growth to bolster your motivation.

Put pen to paper and create an achievable roadmap for change. Time needs to be considered to execute your strategy and get results. Start with the main goals. From there, develop a strategy to reach each goal. Consider the skills you will need and flesh out your roadmap. Once you complete it, you will have more predictability, confidence, and less stress.

Do not cut any corners. You are working to reduce ambiguity. Ask questions throughout the process to gain clarity, reduce the unknown, and identify more opportunities. The more you are aware, the easier it will be to deal with the challenges along the way.

Take advantage of your skills and monitor them as they improve. Notice how you gain efficiencies in your processes. Notice your confidence soar and how easily you are gaining ground.

As you change, notice how your processes change. How you identify, develop solutions, and execute them. Notice how you deal with situations compared to the past. Be proud of personal growth because it is validation you are doing the right things.

Meet change head-on! Match your best skills and values to the desired change. If they do not get you the desired result, then regroup and consider other possibilities to achieve your goal.

Always remain positive! Negativity breeds doubt, but positivity builds confidence. Be positive and consistent in your words, actions, behavior, and motivation. As I explain in my book, Disruption Out of a Box, aligning these elements will produce positive results.

Everyone stumbles along the way and even reaches blockades. Failures are inevitable. "It is not how you fall. It is how you get up." Those immortal words are still being spoken by the immortal Joe

Consider this?!

Namath. And nothing could be more correct. Get up, dust yourself off, gain your composure, regroup, and use your sharpened tools and experience to get what you want.

Do you tend to be lazy? Most people are! If you have concerns about your ability to get the work done, then get an accountability partner. Even better, form a group to meet weekly to openly discuss your challenges. I covered this topic earlier in the book and how you can capitalize on and solve greater problems.

Fifth, a process needs to be developed and adopted to create efficiencies and meaningful results. If it sounds scary, do not worry. Everyone develops and adopts processes, whether they are aware of them or not. It may be as simple as the strategy you use to deal with a difficult relative or co-worker. Or preparing your favorite meal.

In case you find it difficult to develop processes, I am going to share with your basic steps to illuminate what you already know on a subconscious level. Before you dive into them, I recommend you consider a process you already have and get it onto paper. The more times you go through the steps, the more apparent they will become. It will improve your awareness of the steps, and moving forward, creating processes will seem routine.

1. Identify the Process you need and write a description outlining its purpose and benefits.
2. Outline the Scope of the Process. In other words, set boundaries on what it will cover. Include what the process will cover and what it won't cover. Last, specify the limits. When does it begin, and when does it end?
3. Identify the resources you will need. You want to make sure you have what you need and confirm it is a viable solution. Finally, consider the time that goes into the process. Is it worth the effort?
4. Research the unknown. As we learned in the introduction from our lottery winner, a little research goes a long way.

5. Analyze the current situation to address any issues, anything missing, or anything that be improved.
6. Break down each step to the smallest piece possible.
7. Put your steps in order to get the best result.
8. Monitor your performance to determine efficiency, bottlenecks, and other areas for improvement.

Once you know how to efficiently create a process, you will see how it will save you time. As you master each process and adopt them, you will also gain confidence and increasingly better results.

Sixth, you must execute. Executing is where the rubber meets the road! Throughout the book, you have seen how to attack different situations with processes and techniques. It is now time to execute, and it will require your honed skills and a process or plan. You are ready for the task so get excited about the adventure.

One of the skills you need to be mindful of is your ability to manage. I am referring to managing yourself, others, time, and situations. Therefore, you will need to be well organized, track your progress, and ensure overall success. You are the captain of the ship, and the outcome is up to you.

So why not supercharge it all to create even more efficiency? I am talking about delegating or assigning tasks. Dividing your plan or process into segments will insulate you from everything going wrong. Think of it as a stop valve in the middle of a pipe that allows you to stop the flow of the liquid in the pipe. You decide when to release the valve and let the water flow.

By delegating tasks, people will work simultaneously to solve different challenges. The amount of time saved could be proportionate to the total number of tasks. For example, you want to prepare a three-course meal for your friends. You need different ingredients prepared for different dishes. The dishes also need to be prepared and arranged on plates. If you have one person cutting up the food, one cooking, and the other preparing the plates, they can finish faster than one person doing it all. Depending upon the courses, it is possible for all three to be working almost simultaneously and finishing in a third of the time it would take one person.

Here is where your management skills come in. You will need to oversee each person to make certain they do things properly. If two of the three do everything correctly and the other does not, then not all is lost. A correction is made, and the dinner still gets completed in substantially less time than one person doing it all.

The principle still applies even if it is you doing everything. If you break everything into segments, you have an opportunity to check at the end of each segment. In other words, you prepare the ingredients, check them, and put them aside. You then prepare each dish separately and check each dish upon completion. Last, you arrange the food on the plates. To be successful, you will need to manage your skills and time.

As you can see, management is critical. You may not see yourself as a manager, but to be a successful manager, you will need to carefully uplift your management skill. You will be managing people and expectations regardless of whether you are the CEO or Co-Founding Marketing Officer, so get comfortable with the thought.

Seventh, you will get distracted. We all struggle with distractions to some degree, the phone, computer, friends, or our thoughts. Distractions are like motivation. There are two kinds, internal and external. Understanding each will give you an advantage. You will prepare for them and know how to deal with each, so you do not get sidetracked.

First are Internal distractions which are your thoughts and emotions. For example, you only have one hour to finish the task you are working on and then need to pick someone up at the airport. Or you cannot seem to focus because all you are thinking about is your recent breakup with your girlfriend.

A few suggestions to help you manage your internal distractions include the following:

- Consider incorporating a change of scenery. During your breaks by going on a short walk or do an errand.
- Make a daily plan. Schedule time for each task. Work in one-hour blocks and then take a break. Science shows that your ability to focus is significantly better.
- Be mindful of the best time of day to tackle challenging assignments. Consider tackling the most challenging and important tasks first thing in the morning.
- Practice self-regulation to be aware of and control your behaviors and thoughts.
- Find your happy place. In other words, where do you work best? At the park, the office, or your desk at home?
- Physical activity is wonderful for reducing and even eliminating stress.
- Journaling your thoughts is a great practice. It allows you to get the thoughts off your mind to deal with later. You need not worry. You will forget what is plaguing you.
- Implement breathing exercises or music to transition between activities.
- Get at least 7-9 hours of continuous sleep. Whether you need to take melatonin, CBD oil, or whatever else will do the trick, it is imperative to optimal performance.
- Be organized and have important things prioritized. Uncertainty can be draining.

Consider this?!

The second type of distraction is External distractions, ones originating from outside of you. These would include technology, other people, or noise.

- Try using the following tips to minimize or eliminate external distractions.
- Find an environment that has the least distractions.
- Contain potential external distractions such as your phone, alarms, or your computer.

Eighth, be patient. Not everything will be comfortable or smooth sailing. Do not let your patience get the best of you. You can make critical mistakes if you lose your patience. You may offend someone important or damage something. Cooler heads prevail. The following are some tips on how to keep your cool.

- BREATHE! BREATHE! BREATHE! Breathing is always the best place to start. Withholding your breath creates both physical and mental stress, so BREATHE!
- Be an observer. As an observer, you will create space and remove judgment. Rushing to judgment is responsible for many poor decisions. Back away from the situation and breathe. Tell yourself it is only a movie, and don't get emotionally invested. Once you are calm and detached, you can see things for what they are and make better decisions.
- Be aware of stress points. Analyze the situation and find the root cause. Reacting too quickly may not address the underlying problem and only fuel more tension. Positively ask questions.
- You will learn more by listening than speaking. Uncovering problems in a respectful manner will defuse a situation and help everyone resolve the conflict easier.

- Get an objective and valued opinion. We surely do not know everything, so when in doubt, get a second opinion. I previously gave you examples of how certainty reduces stress. Here is another opportunity.
- Don't run away from being responsible for yourself.

As an entrepreneur, you are also a leader. The next time your patience is put to the test, use it as an opportunity to evaluate your purpose, vulnerability, and maturity as a leader. The more patience you practice, the more resourceful, composed, compassionate, and mindful you will become as a leader.

Ninth, frequent affirmations of your beliefs have significant benefits.

They are powerful and have an incredibly positive effect on our lives. The following benefits will help you tremendously as an entrepreneur and in your personal life:

- Elevated Self Esteem & Self Confidence
- Reduce Stress & Anxiety
- Elevated Positive Thinking
- Improved Relationships
- Improved Mental Health
- Improved Sleep
- Improved Focus & Performance
- Help Us Achieve Our Goals
- Elevated Happiness & Positivity
- Improve Ability to Overcome Negative Thought Patterns

Your Guide

How To Become A Successful Entrepreneur

"Managing your time makes it easier to manage your life."

-Steven Griffith-

Four years ago, I was in Mexico and connected with my friend Ryan who happened to come to town for a visit. We are talking about setting up a business and how to capitalize on efficiencies. During the conversation, he mentioned one of his friends, Steven Griffith, who is also a client.

Steven recently published his book, The Time Cleanse: A Proven System to Eliminate Wasted Time, Realize Your Full Potential, and Reinvest in What Matters Most. We jumped on a call and spoke with Steven. Immediately, I decided to meet with Steven upon my return to Los Angeles. I needed to learn more about his thoughts on time management.

When I returned to Los Angeles, I reached out to Steven and suggested we meet. He agreed and also offered to attend his workshop in a few weeks. The workshop was designed to show people how to capitalize on the knowledge from his book. I was excited at the prospect and agreed to attend.

I showed up to the event early. It was at a prominent social club in Orange County. There were tables and chairs set up in a large banquet hall for the day-long event. I mingled with successful people across many business sectors, and we then took our seats.

The following seven hours proved to be one of the most enlightening days. Steven went through his book, bringing awareness to the audience at each step. It was shocking to see how even successful people could be so poor at managing their time.

I mentioned earlier that time is a critical factor in success. You can create a roadmap to reach your goal with benchmarks along the way in increments measured by time. However, that is not enough!

To reach your goal, you need to be aware of time and manage it well. During Steven's event, the audience participated in an exercise. We all answered a series of questions, and each question was tied to an amount of time. When we reached the end of the questions, we were asked to total up all of the time from the questions.

What followed was shocking! Steven then asked people randomly to share the total amount of time they were wasting or misappropriating over a week. Keep in mind that the average person in the room worked from 40 to 72 hours per week.

As we went around the room, people shared their numbers, the hours per week they worked, hours wasted, and hours misappropriated. The first gentleman replied, 50 hours of work, 16 hours wasted, and 8 hours misappropriated. In other words, 24 of his 50 hours spent working, or half were of little to no value. And yet he was still financially successful. Can you imagine how much more successful he could be?

The results showed everyone why they were finding their financial goal elusive. Results varied as we went around the room, but it was clear how we all waste and misappropriated time. Unbelievably, there were people with even worse numbers.

My numbers were among the lowest, but even I was wasting 6 hours a week and misappropriating another 6 hours, roughly 20% of my work time. It made me question my priorities and habits. If you want to learn how much time you are wasting or misappropriating and how to improve your efficiency at work, I highly recommend you read The Time Cleanse: A Proven System to Eliminate Wasted Time, Realize Your Full Potential, and Reinvest in What Matters Most.

Yes, time is a constant. It does not change. Therefore, if you set goals tied to a timeline, then execution is everything. You will need to remain mindful of the time and the things that are slowing you down. Those things can be your plan, processes, and even your habits.

I have shared how to address these matters previously. Before you commence to achieve a goal, you need to take a hard look at your skills your see if they match up with your timeline. In other words, based on your skills, you will achieve your goals in the timeframes you have chosen.

If the answer is yes, you are in good shape. If the answer is no, then you need to do one of two things. Your first option is to improve the skills that are deficient in meeting your deadlines. Or the second option, recruit others with the skills necessary to complete the challenging things to save time.

At this point, it should be clear that being a successful entrepreneur takes a great deal. You need, among other things, awareness, a plan, skills, hard work, and results. The journey can be interesting, fun, and enlightening, or it can be challenging, draining, and a trip you cannot wait to finish. Your mindset is the difference.

My goal is to hear of your success. I want you to be excited about what you are doing and internally motivated to learn and succeed. You have what you need to complete your puzzle. If you feel otherwise, then all you need is to work on your skills.

It is now time to plan your path to success. You are the one who has the goal, the tools, the plan, and the motivation. All I can do is be your guide. You will need to chop wood and carry water. You are the hurdler about to set your feet in the blocks before you sprint for the finish line.

The following is what I can share to keep you in your lane, determined, and confident. Yet, it is ultimately up to you to finish the race because neither I nor anyone else will be allowed to set foot on the track. Get ready and remember, if you want to win, you will need to give it your best.

It is now time to consider this:

1. What is your goal?
2. Why do you want to do it?
3. How much does it mean to you to achieve it?
4. Do you believe you can achieve it?
5. What do you possess that will make it possible to achieve?
6. How will you reach your goal?
7. What is necessary for you to reach your goal?
8. What will success look like?

Do you know what each of these questions represents? Can you properly answer each one of them? If not, you have not done the work. And, if you kid yourself into thinking you are confident about each of your answers, and they are wrong, the truth will soon be revealed.

Earlier I said I wanted to hear about your success. It is the truth! I do not want to lessen your chance for success by keeping you guessing or doubting. A good coach builds you up and sends you out with confidence. And that is what I am going to do in these final pages.

You have your Goal. It is personal to you. You see it clearly. Speak it aloud! Feel the elevation of your emotions. Tell me what you are feeling. If you feel nothing, then keep repeating the goal aloud until you feel your emotions kick in.

Remember the elevated feeling when you hear yourself speak of your goal. Tell me the reason you Desire to reach the Goal. Include every detail you can. Take your time and enjoy the process.

Tell me on the deepest level possible your Motivation. In other words, what it means to reach the goal? You will need to remember your answer. Keep it short, and be sure it is the honest answer. You will need the answer when you meet bigger challenges along the way. Write it down!

Examine your beliefs or thoughts on the goal. Examine your beliefs about yourself. Tell me the reason you can achieve the goal.

Convince me you can do it. Tell me what Values you have that will make it possible to achieve them. I want to know specifically the hard and soft skills you plan to put to use. Tell me the other resources you will employ.

Explain to me the level of organization you have to get the job done. Give me the details on the processes and techniques you plan to implement to reach your Goal. Share your confidence with me.

Tell me the Action you will take to execute your plan. Additionally, explain to me the things you will rely upon when you face challenges. In other words, as you are chopping wood and carrying water, the axe may get dull, and the bucket spring holes.

You have learned many techniques in the book. Share the ones you have mastered and intend to use to overcome challenges. Make certain you are confident in your abilities to get the job done. Tell with no uncertainty you will not be the scuba diver panicking on the ceiling.

If you complete everything I have asked of you, then you are ready to succeed. You have completed the necessary steps to achieve your goal. I know because you shared your goal aloud.

Further, you shared your Desire and the feelings you felt. You know the feeling associated with achieving your goal. You now have an internal reference.

Your motivation is clear. It is internal. It is your greatest weapon. It is more powerful than money or anything else material. You can reflect on it and draw strength from it. When you reach a tipping point, you will clear any hurdle.

You have confidence. Your beliefs are solid, and you can achieve your goal. No one will persuade you otherwise. The work has been done, and you are ready.

The tools in your toolbox are sharp. Your SWOT analysis is complete, and you have addressed your weaknesses and threats. You know what is important and the Values you will maintain to achieve success. Nothing can stop you.

Your plan is etched in stone. Unknowns have been minimized or eliminated. The roadmap includes the benchmarks you need to keep you focused. You have structure and the tools to execute.

Training is complete! Game day is here, and you are ready to spring into action. You also have awareness, information, knowledge, and wisdom on your side. You are perfectly aligned. Nothing can stop you from reaching your goal.

Closing Thought

It was the summer of 1979 in Austin, Texas. I was at my cousin's house in the middle of the night, partying with Stevie Ray Vaughn and the band after one of their performances at a local bar.

Stevie Ray was sitting on the couch next to me, fiddling with his guitar. We are all chatting away and sharing thoughts. I was undecided about my career and my life, uncomfortable, and candidly miserable.

I finished my bitching and complaining and fell back in my chair, exhausted and disgusted. Stevie Ray casually stops picking, pauses for a moment, and leans over, double taps me on the leg, and with a shake of the head and big smile, rolls the words, "Listen cuz, we all have greatness. We just have to let it out."

You, too, have greatness! *"It is now your turn; so just let it out."*

Glossary

Asbestos — Asbestos is the name given to a group of naturally occurring fibrous minerals that are resistant to heat and corrosion.

Audioception — The sense of sound perception.

Axons — The long threadlike part of a nerve cell along which impulses are conducted from the cell body to other cells.

Block Universe Theory — The universe is a giant block of all the things that ever happen at any time and any place. On this view, the past, present, and future all exist — and are equally real.

Boson — A subatomic particle, such as a photon, has zero or integral spin and follows the statistical description of S. N. Bose and Einstein.

Caudate nucleus — A paired, "C"-shaped subcortical structure which lies deep inside the brain near the thalamus.

Cerebral cortex — The outer layer that lies on top of your cerebrum.

Chemoreception — The ability to perceive specific chemical stimuli is one of the most evolutionarily ancient forms of interaction between living organisms and their environment.

Clairaudience — The supposed faculty of perceiving, as if by hearing, what is inaudible.

Clairvoyance	The supposed faculty of perceiving things or events in the future or beyond normal sensory contact.
Cortisol	The primary stress hormone increases sugars (glucose) in the bloodstream, enhances your brain's use of glucose, and increases the availability of substances that repair tissues.
Cutaneous Reception	The type of sensory receptor found in the skin (the dermis or epidermis).
Diethylstibestrol	A synthetic form of the hormone estrogen that was prescribed to pregnant women between about 1940 and 1971 because it was thought to prevent miscarriages.
Dopamine	It is known as the "feel-good" hormone. It gives you a sense of pleasure.
Echoic memory	It is the ultra-short-term memory for things you hear.
Electro-chemical reactions	It is a process in which electrons flow between a solid electrode and substance, such as an electrolyte.
Endorphins	They are chemicals (hormones) your body releases when it feels pain or stress.
Equilibrioception	It refers to a combination of processes by which an organism can perceive its orientation with respect to gravity.
Flow State	It describes a feeling where, under the right conditions, you become fully immersed in whatever you are doing.

Glucocorticoids	They are corticosteroids that bind to the glucocorticoid receptor that is present in almost every vertebrate animal cell.
Gustaoception	Taste (gustaoception) refers to the ability to detect substances such as food, certain minerals, poisons, etc.
Haptic memory	This type of memory is related to your sense of touch.
Hypothalamus	A structure deep in your brain acts as the body's smart control coordination center.
Interoceptors	A sensory receptor that receives stimuli from within the body, especially from the gut and other internal organs.
Kinesthetic Sense	The senses of position and movement of the body senses we are aware of only on introspection.
KPI (Key Performance Indicator)	These are targets that help you measure progress against your most strategic objectives.
Law of Attraction	It states that whatever you focus your energy on will come back to you.
Macro-flow	It is a powerful software tool for rapid and accurate flow and thermal design of flow systems in a wide variety of engineering applications.
Mechanoreceptors	They are a type of somatosensory receptors that relay extracellular stimulus to intracellular signal transduction through mechanically gated ion channels.
Melatonin	It is a hormone that your brain produces in response to darkness. It helps with the timing

	of your circadian rhythms (24-hour internal clock) and with sleep.
Methylphenidate	Used to treat children with attention deficit hyperactivity disorder (ADHD). It helps with hyperactivity and impulsive behavior and allows them to concentrate better.
Micro-flow	The flow of fluid through a microscale device.
Nociception	It refers to the central nervous system (CNS) and peripheral nervous system (PNS) processing of noxious stimuli, such as tissue injury and temperature extremes, which activate nociceptors and their pathways.
Olfacoception	The sense of smell.
Ophthalmoception	It is the ability of the eye(s) to focus and detect images of visible light on photoreceptors in the retina that generate electrical nerve impulses for varying colors, hues, and brightness.
Osteoporosis	A medical condition in which the bones become brittle and fragile from loss of tissue, typically as a result of hormonal changes or deficiency of calcium or vitamin D.
Oxytocin	A hormone released by the pituitary gland that causes increased contraction of the uterus during labor and stimulates the ejection of milk into the ducts of the breasts.
Photons	A tiny particle that comprises waves of electromagnetic radiation.
Platonia	A small genus of South American timber trees (family Guttiferae) with opposite pinnate veined leaves and showy, usually solitary

	terminal roseate flowers that are followed by globose edible single-seeded berries see bacury.
Precognition	Foreknowledge of an event, especially as a form of extrasensory perception.
Prefrontal cortex	The gray matter of the anterior part of the frontal lobe that is highly developed in humans and plays a role in the regulation of complex cognitive, emotional, and behavioral functioning.
Premonition	A strong feeling that something is about to happen, especially something unpleasant.
Proprioception	Perception or awareness of the position and movement of the body.
Quantum Chromodynamics	It is the theory of the strong interaction between quarks mediated by gluons.
Quantum Field Theory	Body of physical principles combining the elements of quantum mechanics with those of relativity to explain the behavior of subatomic particles and their interactions via a variety of force fields.
Recovery (Flow)	Stages happen in sleep, where the experience can be integrated, and real learning takes place.
Release (Flow)	Stage happens when you take your mind off of the situation. As you detach and let go, you become an observer of the situation.
Resonance	A phenomenon in which an external force or a vibrating system forces another system around it to vibrate with greater amplitude at a specified frequency of operation..

Sensory memory	It is the perception of sight, hearing, smell, taste, and touch information entering through the sensory cortices of the brain and relaying through the thalamus.
Serotonin	It is a chemical that carries messages between nerve cells in the brain and throughout your body.
String theory	Theory proposes that the fundamental constituents of the universe are one-dimensional "strings" rather than point-like particles.
Struggle (Flow)	In the struggle stage, you are in over your head and out of control. The situation is beyond your current capacity to handle.
Subcortex	It is where we process more primitive functions (e.g., emotion processed in the amygdala).
Sulpiride	Sulpiride is a substituted benzamide derivative, and a selective dopamine D2 antagonist indicated to treat acute and chronic schizophrenia.
SWOT	Strengths, Weaknesses, Opportunities, and Threats
Tactility	The condition of being tactile (relating to or able to be perceived by the sense of touch).
Tactioception	Touch or somatosensation (tactioception, tactition, or mechanoreception) is a perception resulting from the activation of neural receptors in the skin, including hair follicles, tongue, throat, and mucosa.
Telepathy	The supposed communication of thoughts or ideas by means other than the known senses.

Thermoception	Thermoception refers to temperature sensation.
Tryptophan	It is an amino acid needed for normal growth in infants and for the production and maintenance of the body's proteins, muscles, enzymes, and neurotransmitters.

Notations

1. https://en.wikipedia.org/wiki/Quark
2. https://en.wikipedia.org/wiki/Gluon
3. https://ourworldindata.org/marriages-and-divorces
4. https://bodytomy.com/how-many-senses-does-human-have
5. https://www.who.int/news-room/questions-and-answers/item/nutrition-trans-fat
6. https://www.abc.net.au/news/science/2018-09-02/block-universe-theory-time-past-present-future-travel/10178386
7. https://en.wikipedia.org/wiki/Plymouth_Rock
8. https://www.sciencedaily.com/releases/2021/12/211217102743.htm
9. https://aiimpacts.org/information-storage-in-the-brain/
10. https://www.psychreg.org/dennis-relojo-howell/
11. https://www.verywellmind.com/classical-conditioning-2794859
12. https://www.flowresearchcollective.com
13. https://engineering.mit.edu/engage/ask-an-engineer/what-are-thoughts-made-of/
14. https://reimaginingeducation.org/what-is-resonance-energy-transfer-in-photosynthesis/
15. https://en.wikipedia.org/wiki/Resonance

16. https://the-quark.com/neuralink-explained-elon-musks-brain-chip/
17. https://en.wikipedia.org/wiki/String_theory
18. https://en.wikipedia.org/wiki/Law_of_attraction_(New_Thought)
19. https://www.scalarlight.com/blog/article/quantum-field-theory-explained
20. https://www.sci.news/physics/science-stephen-hawking-black-holes-information-03172.html
21. https://www.nih.gov/news-events/nih-research-matters/dopamine-affects-how-brain-decides-whether-goal-worth-effort#:~:text=Previous%20studies%20have%20shown%20that%20increases%20in%20dopamine,whether%20a%20mental%20task%20is%20worth%20the%20effort.
22. https://www.medicalnewstoday.com/articles/320839
23. https://www.psycom.net/oxytocin
24. https://my.clevelandclinic.org/health/articles/22572serotonin#:~:text=Serotonin%20is%20a%20chemical%20that,blood%20clotting%20and%20sexual%20desire
25. https://my.clevelandclinic.org/health/articles/22187-cortisol
26. https://en.wikipedia.org/wiki/Robert_Downey_Jr.
27. http://www.amazon.co.uk/The-Top-Five-Regrets-Dying/dp/1848509995/ref=sr_1_1?ie=UTF8&qid=1367096226&sr=8-1&keywords=top+regrets+of+the+dying

LEARN MORE ABOUT KEITH HERMAN

- Keith Herman *https://www.keithherman.com*
- Funding & Disrupting Podcast *https://fundingdisrupting.com*
- LinkedIn *https://www.linkedin.com/in/keithherman1/*
- Twitter *https://twitter.com/KeithHerman1111*

For information about exclusive discounts for bulk purchases, engagements, or general inquiries please contact Keith Publishing at business@keithherman.com.

www.ingramcontent.com/pod-product-compliance
Lightning Source LLC
Chambersburg PA
CBHW071310110426
42743CB00042B/1251